Job Man

Job Man

My Life in Professional Wrestling

Chris Multerer
with Larry Widen

Foreword by Baron von Raschke

WISCONSIN HISTORICAL SOCIETY PRESS

Published by the Wisconsin Historical Society Press
Publishers since 1855

The Wisconsin Historical Society helps people connect to the past by col-
lecting, preserving, and sharing stories. Founded in 1846, the Society is one
of the nation's finest historical institutions.
Join the Wisconsin Historical Society: wisconsinhistory.org/membership

Back cover photo by Larry Widen

Printed in the United States of America
Cover design by Steve Biel
Typesetting by Wendy Holdman

23 22 21 20 19   1 2 3 4 5

Library of Congress Cataloging-in-Publication Data
Names: Multerer, Chris, author. | Widen, Larry, author. | Baron von
    Raschke, writer of foreword.
Title: Job man : my life in professional wrestling / by Chris Multerer with
    Larry Widen ; foreword by Baron von Raschke.
Description: [Madison] : Wisconsin Historical Society Press, [2019]
Identifiers: LCCN 2019017459| ISBN 9780870209253 (pbk.) |
    ISBN 9780870209260 (ebk.)
Subjects: LCSH: Multerer, Chris. | Wrestlers—United States—Biography.
Classification: LCC GV1196.M84 A3 2019 | DDC 796.812092 [B]—dc23
    LC record available at https://lccn.loc.gov/2019017459

♾ The paper used in this publication meets the minimum requirements of
the American National Standard for Information Sciences—Permanence of
Paper for Printed Library Materials, ANSI Z39.48-1992.

Contents

Foreword

There's an old saying in the wrestling business that some fans—and a few wrestlers—don't know the difference between a wristlock and wristwatch. There are those who don't know the difference between a jabroni and a Zamboni. You probably don't care one way or the other. But after reading *Job Man* by Chris Multerer, you'll realize the importance of the men on the undercard television matches who unselfishly helped make others wrestling stars.

There are a lot of facets to professional wrestling, such as the hoopla created on TV by the promoters, announcers, referees, and finally, the wrestlers. All of this is done to get the fans out of the comfort of their living rooms and into the arenas.

Job Man focuses on those reliable people who drove the many miles through all kinds of weather to make television wrestling a success. One week, the jobbers came from their homes in Winnipeg, Ontario; the next week, from Chicago; and the week after that, from Milwaukee. Five or six guys piled into a car and drove several hundred miles to a television studio in Minneapolis just to wrestle as hard as they could for a few minutes to highlight another wrestler's talent. They split the expenses and often crowded into one motel room to save money. On the trip back, they talked about the matches they had, played cards, and repeated the stories they heard from the old-timers: the myths and legends of the sport—and the job—they loved.

Some of the jobbers were hoping to be discovered, and a

few were, but only after years of hard work. My very good friend and mentor, Maurice Vachon, struggled for fourteen years in the Oregon territory before promoter Don Owens realized what a talent he had working for him. After one of Maurice's undercard matches in Portland broke out in a riot, the police came in and cleared the building. A very angry Owens approached Maurice and exclaimed, "You were like a mad dog out there!" When things cooled down, the wrestler and promoter had a meeting, and a star was born. His name was Mad Dog Vachon. Mad Dog sold out houses in Owens's territory for many years afterward.

Roddy Piper was part of the Winnipeg gang that taped matches at the Calhoun Beach Hotel television studios every third Saturday until he broke into the big time as "Rowdy" Roddy Piper. When I first met Jerry Blackwell, he was doing jobs on the Charlotte, North Carolina, television network. He went on to become "Crusher" Jerry Blackwell, one of the best wrestlers in the business.

My hat is off to the very talented, hardworking men who helped me so much in the course of my career, and I thank them sincerely. Now, sit back and get comfortable. Let your mind enter the locker room with Chris Multerer as you read his story.

—*Baron von Raschke, "The Claw"*

Introduction

I've known Chris Multerer since 1973, and while I didn't think about it at the time, it seems perfectly natural that we'd still be friends more than forty years later. How can you not love a guy who knows his Three Stooges backward and forward? A guy who can con you into seeing a movie called *Dr. Tarr's Torture Dungeon*? Or a guy who loves professional wrestling so much that he made a career of it? The answer is you can't, especially if they're all the same person.

One night, Chris was driving around the town square in Baraboo, Wisconsin, when a policeman pulled him over for driving the wrong way on a one-way street. "Have you been drinking, Christopher?" the officer asked. "No, I'm from Milwaukee!" was the reply. So when Chris asked if I'd help him with his autobiography, you can see why it took me almost one whole second to say yes. As with everything else we've done together over the last four-plus decades, it was a blast.

I was with Chris when he wrestled a six-hundred-pound bear at the Milwaukee Sentinel Sports Show. I was in that drafty old ballroom on Fond du Lac Avenue when he stepped inside a ring for the very first time. And I was there when he worked a superstar opponent at the Milwaukee Arena less than a year later. We'd attended pro wrestling cards there before, but on that day in 1979, I saw the whole thing from a different vantage. After Chris's match, I found myself watching the fans as they lived, for a moment, inside the drama playing itself out before their eyes.

The most enthusiastic of them came to life when the babyface was pummeling the heel and sank back in their seats when the actions were reversed. In particular, I've never forgotten a woman who was oblivious to everything except what was happening inside the ring.

"Break his arm, break his arm," she hollered at the top of her lungs. "Break it off!" Milwaukee's favorite son, the Crusher, was attempting to do exactly that, running the heel face-first into the turnbuckle before finishing him off with a resounding blow from the one-hundred-megaton bicep that we'd seen during TV interviews. After the decision, the Crusher walked the circumference of the ring and acknowledged the applause from his fans. He stepped through the ropes and began to make his way toward the dressing room. When he saw the woman jump from her seat, he leaned in and gave her a hug. As the Crusher moved away, she turned back to the ring where the heel was regaining consciousness. "That'll teach ya," she screeched. "Go home, ya lousy bum!" The woman wasn't the only one venting her feelings that night. More than a few glasses of beer and tubs of popcorn hit the floor because their owners were swept up in the excitement as two three-hundred-pound athletes tried to pound one another into submission.

This was the world of professional wrestling, where the violent, choreographed ballet boiled down to the good guys against the bad guys. Sometimes justice prevailed, sometimes not. If it didn't, the fans simply had to try again next month. Marty O'Neill, the beloved announcer on television's *All-Star Wrestling*, used to close out the broadcast by saying, "Run, don't walk, to the box office and get your tickets now." Sales for the house shows were fueled by Marty's on-camera interviews with the wrestlers. Lord Alfred Hayes, a heel who spoke with a bad British accent, told Milwaukee wrestling fans their town was the worst he'd ever seen. "The beer is warm, the women are cold, and the Packers stink," Hayes said. After that, who wouldn't buy a ticket to see the Crusher clean dat bum's snooty English clock? In those days, a family of four could enjoy hot dogs and soft drinks while sitting thirty feet from the ring, all for about thirty-five dollars, maybe forty if the old man had a couple of beers. And even if they weren't sitting near her, they certainly experienced the fun of a fire-breathing wrestling expert whose volume rose incrementally during the next match. "Throw him over the ropes," she bellowed. "Poke him in the eyes!"

—Larry Widen

Chapter 1

As I write this book, I'm in my sixties, and if I sit too long in one position, invariably a few aches and pains remind me of the days when I put over main-event wrestlers such as Reggie Lisowski, Mad Dog Vachon, and Hulk Hogan. In my role as a job man, those guys looked like the superstar entertainers they worked so hard to become. Yes, pro wrestlers are entertainers. Pro wrestlers are also storytellers. And, perhaps more than anything else, they are athletes. Every competent wrestler has the ability to seriously injure his or her opponent. The skill in professional wrestling is learning to take potentially dangerous falls in such a way as to render them harmless. One wrong move and you're in a wheelchair for life.

I speak from experience. During my career, I've dislocated my knees more times than I can count. I've torn a rotator cuff in my shoulder, broken a hand, cracked a few ribs, bruised a kidney, and split my head wide open. Yet, if I could, I'd go back and do it all over again because I feel like the luckiest guy in the world. I had the time of my life wrestling in nearly seven hundred matches all over the United States. Not many people can look back on a career and honestly say they loved what they did for a living.

When my friend and longtime professional wrestler Bobby "the Brain" Heenan died in September 2017, it reminded me of our time in the ring together. Heenan, along with Ray "the Crippler" Stevens, inspired me to get into professional wrestling. Heenan did some of the most entertaining television interviews ever and was one of the greatest ring performers in the history of the sport. Heenan was Nick Bockwinkel's manager when I refereed matches between the Crusher and Bockwinkel, Wahoo McDaniel and Bockwinkel, and Big Bad Bobby Duncum and Tito Santana. When I failed to catch or notice Heenan interfering with his matches, the crowds always went berserk. Heenan brought so much heat on me as a referee that I often needed the police or sheriff to escort me to my car and get me safely out of town. Bobby Heenan was the best.

Most people might not realize it, but professional wrestling is a form of art. Equal parts theater and storytelling, pro wrestling is about good versus evil, heroes against villains, and justice triumphing over injustice. It is the job of every wrestler to make the crowd feel like they are part of the action.

For me, the dream of getting in on the action in professional wrestling started in suburban Brookfield, Wisconsin, in 1966. At the time, I was living with my grandfather, Elmer Rulf, near Capitol Drive and Calhoun Road. One hot summer night in August, my parents, Ronald and Barbara, were relaxing with my grandfather in the backyard. My brothers and I were horsing around, throwing a ball at each other and laughing our butts off. When I threw a fastball at my brother Dennis, he ducked and the baseball hit my sister in the back. She started crying, and my old man sent me in the house, where I was told to sit on the couch and think about what I'd done. Fat chance of that happening! I was nine years old and upset that I wasn't outside having fun with the others. I turned on the TV and started flipping channels to see if there was anything to watch.

In those days, there were only six or seven channels, and half of them were public broadcasting. When I came across the American Wrestling Association (AWA)'s *All-Star Wrestling*, the professional wrestling show put on by Verne Gagne and broadcast in Milwaukee on Channel 18, one of the UHF stations, I paused. I watched, mesmerized by guys such as Dick the Bruiser, the

With my mom, Barbara, my dad, Ron, brothers Tim and Dennis, and my sister, Cindy, in 1978. LARRY WIDEN

Crusher, Johnny Valentine, Pat O'Connor, and Wilbur Snyder as they tossed each other around the ring. What really got my attention, though, were the heels, or the bad guys. Heels such as Mad Dog Vachon, Mitsu Arakawa, and a few others had distinctive, over-the-top personalities.

When my parents came into the house to see if I was sorry for hitting my sister with a fastball, they found me glued to the television. The fact that I was watching wrestling made them even madder! My mom hated the violence in the ring, along with the yelling and bragging and posturing that went on when wrestlers were interviewed as part of the show.

One day my mom came into the room while I was watching wrestling. The Crusher was doing an interview to hype his feud with Kobayashi. The Crusher had a garbage can, and he growled, "I'm gonna pack dat bum in dis can and ship him back to Tokyo." That was the last straw for Mom. "No more of that," she said,

Joseph Maurice Régis Vachon was born in Canada in 1929. As a child, he followed the professional wrestling matches in Montréal and began training after he saw a comic book ad for a wrestling school near his home. By age fourteen, he was training regularly at the YMCA and working as a stevedore on the docks. Vachon was chosen to compete as an amateur wrestler at the 1948 Olympic Games in London, ultimately finishing in seventh place. Although his dream of winning at the Olympics failed to materialize, Vachon met American champion wrestler Verne Gagne, who convinced him to turn pro.

Vachon began wrestling on the Canadian circuit in 1951 but was unable to distinguish himself from the many other athletes like himself who were doing the same thing. Vachon worked in the gym to add fifty pounds of muscle to his 175-pound frame. He then shaved his head, grew a long goatee, and renamed himself Mad Dog Vachon. He went to Texas and wrestled as a heel with great success. By the time he began wrestling out of Portland, Oregon, Vachon was one of the sport's most hated villains. He recruited his younger brother, Paul who wrestled as Butcher Vachon, to become his tag team partner. Together, the Vachons gained a reputation as the most fearsome team of rule-breakers in the business. In 1962, Gagne hired the Vachons to work for the AWA. The feud between Gagne and Mad Dog Vachon was legendary and stretched on for twenty years. Mad Dog and Butcher also had a long-running feud with the Crusher and Dick the Bruiser that included a famous steel cage match at Chicago's Comiskey Park.

In 1987, Vachon was struck by a hit-and-run driver while jogging in Iowa. The injury resulted in the amputation of one of his legs, ending his career in the ring. Because of his inimitable, snarling voice, Vachon was able to do interviews, ringside commentary, and television commercials until the end of his life. He died in 2013.

snapping the television off. "I don't want any more of that crud coming into this house!" No problem, I thought. When you're nine years old, you find a way around any little setback. Besides, I could usually convince my dad to let me watch wrestling if Mom wasn't around.

Toward the end of 1966, our family moved from my grandfather's house in Brookfield to our own place in Milwaukee. I soon found that while it was fun being in the city, the move introduced a big problem. The little black-and-white television set we had didn't pick up *All-Star Wrestling* on Channel 18 without the addition of a circular wire UHF antenna. My parents couldn't have been happier. They didn't like me watching wrestling, so they refused to add the antenna.

My parents should have known that I wasn't about to let a little thing like an antenna keep me from watching wrestling. Kohl's department store on Appleton Avenue was only three blocks away from my new house. A whole section in that store was devoted to television sets. So, every Saturday evening at five o'clock, I went to Kohl's and sat there for an hour watching wrestling. I never called attention to myself, so the salesmen were pretty cool about my being there. I think a couple of them liked the fact that a shopper was watching wrestling. That way, the salesmen could justify keeping it on. When the show ended, I went straight home in time for dinner. I was never late, and my folks never wondered where I went every Saturday night. Luckily, my parents never went shopping at Kohl's while I was there!

Needless to say, I was hooked. Verne Gagne's *All-Star Wrestling* offered viewers a chance to see the best wrestlers in the business compete against each other. Gagne's inexpensive, locally produced television show was syndicated in major cities such as Minneapolis, Milwaukee, Chicago, Omaha, Winnipeg, and Denver, as well as in smaller markets such as Green Bay, Rockford, and Duluth. In addition to instantly making household names out of Gagne, Dr. Bill Miller, Larry "the Axe" Hennig, Baron von Raschke, and others, *All-Star Wrestling* was an hour-long advertisement for the AWA's house shows in those cities. Gagne himself was a major draw. He had wrestled for the University of Minnesota in the 1940s, winning two National Collegiate Athletic Association (NCAA) wrestling titles while also playing football for the Golden Gophers. Later, in 1960, he started the AWA with Wally Karbo and was a fixture in the sport for decades.

Gagne knew how to entertain and give fans what they wanted. For example, I remember when, in 1967, a guy with a paper bag on his head issued a challenge to Gagne, who was at the time the AWA heavyweight champion. Gagne refused to acknowledge the

Longtime AWA owner and promoter Wally Karbo was born in Minneapolis in 1915. The Great Depression was on when Karbo graduated from high school, and he immediately went to work full time for the Minneapolis Boxing and Wrestling Club as an assistant to owner Tony Stecher. Over the next twenty years, Karbo learned all aspects of the business, especially the booking and promoting of fighters. In 1952, Karbo was offered the chance to buy a one-third interest in the club. In 1959, Verne Gagne bought out the other partners, making himself and Karbo the owners. They changed the name of the club to the American Wrestling Association and focused on developing professional wrestlers for shows in the Midwest.

Karbo booked job men from Milwaukee, Chicago, and Winnipeg for the weekly television show tapings. He also booked them for opening matches and battle royals at the house shows.

Karbo and Gagne were partners for more than thirty years. In 1985, at age eighty, Karbo sold his interest in the AWA to Gagne. Ray Stevens and Blackjack Lanza assumed responsibility for many of his booking duties. Karbo died in 1993.

guy at first, but the challenges went on for a few weeks. Finally, the challenger, who by this time was being called the Masked Man, jumped in the ring during one of Gagne's television matches with Jack Pesek. The Masked Man hit Gagne from behind and put him in a submission hold—the figure-four leglock. While Gagne was writhing in agony, the Masked Man ripped the paper bag from his head to reveal a black mask with an X on the forehead. Because Gagne was unable to continue, the match against Pesek was ruled a no contest. Meanwhile, the Masked Man, who was now calling himself Dr. X, gloated at ringside.

An angry Verne Gagne appeared on camera afterward for an interview with Marty O'Neill, the ringside announcer. Gagne said

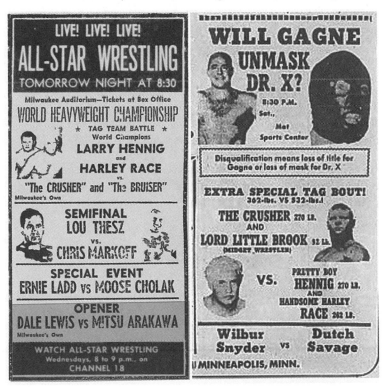

Newspaper advertising made me even more determined to watch wrestling on TV every chance I got. Ultimately, I ended up working with the Crusher, Verne Gagne, Ernie Ladd, and Wilbur Snyder. AMERICAN WRESTLING ASSOCIATION

he would wrestle Dr. X anywhere, anytime. The hype on *All-Star Wrestling* motivated huge numbers of fans to buy tickets to the live events featuring matches between Gagne and Dr. X. The big attendance figures were a testament to Gagne's popularity and to his knowledge of the business. It was Gagne who brought Dr. X— played by wrestler Dick Beyer—to the AWA. As usual, Gagne's move paid off, as Dr. X remained a major draw in the AWA for years.

As part owner of the AWA, Gagne did more as a businessman than as a wrestler to get people interested in professional wrestling and to make money. For example, when Gagne's feud with Dr. X ran its course, Gagne created an angle that pitted Dr. X against the Crusher. After a few weeks of selling the match on *All-Star Wrestling,* the Crusher went up against Dr. X in the main event at a house show in St. Paul. Dr. X won the match, which set the scene for a second confrontation a month later.

AUGUST 26, 1967, ST. PAUL AUDITORIUM— ST. PAUL, MINNESOTA

Dr. X beat the Crusher
Johnny Powers beat Mighty Igor Vodik
Larry Hennig beat Chris Markoff
Al Kashey beat Steve Druk
Harley Race beat Chris Markoff
Rock Rogowski beat Steve Stanlee

SEPTEMBER 9, 1967, ST. PAUL AUDITORIUM— ST. PAUL, MINNESOTA

Dr. X beat the Crusher (disqualification [DQ])
Ramon Torres beat Harley Race
Larry Hennig beat Al Kashey
Rock Rogowski beat the Big K
Chris Markoff beat Steve Druk
Eddie Sharkey beat Paul Caruso

Fans in Moline, Omaha, Duluth, Chicago, Minneapolis, and Winnipeg flocked to the arenas when the feud between Dr. X and the Crusher came to town. Occasionally, the Crusher wasn't available. At a show in Milwaukee in August 1967, for example, Dr. X wrestled Dick the Bruiser. That match ended in disqualification when Dick the Bruiser accidentally knocked out referee Marty Miller. The rematch between Dr. X and Dick the Bruiser, held in Milwaukee in November, was ruled a no contest by Miller when, at the fifteen-minute time limit, the Crusher and Dr. X were still battling outside the ring.

Eventually, the angle between Dr. X and the Crusher played itself out. By the time it did, Dr. X had become the biggest heel in the AWA. Having his name on a card was good for attendance. Gagne capitalized on Dr. X's popularity by booking him in a match against Victor, a six-hundred-pound black bear, on November 25, 1967. The auditorium sold out immediately, and thousands of people who couldn't get tickets waited outside hoping to get in. Victor the Bear won when Dr. X was disqualified.

On April 4, 1971, I finally got to experience all the excitement of pro wrestling in person. My grandpa Jacob surprised me with tickets to a show at the Milwaukee Auditorium. Even though my parents weren't crazy about my love for wrestling, Grandpa knew

---

NOVEMBER 25, 1967, ST. PAUL AUDITORIUM— ST. PAUL, MINNESOTA

Verne Gagne beat Harley Race

Cowboy Bill Watts and Rock Rogowski beat Mitsu Arakawa and Dr. Moto

Victor the Bear beat Dr. X (DQ)

Mighty Igor Vodik beat Blackjack Daniels

The Big K beat Jack Pesek

Mark Starr beat Ken Yates

My grandfather, Jacob Multerer, took me to my first pro wrestling match in April 1971. CHRIS MULTERER

APRIL 7, 1971, MILWAUKEE AUDITORIUM—
MILWAUKEE, WISCONSIN

Larry Hennig and Lars Anderson beat Hercules Cortez and
Haystack Calhoun
Bull Bullinski beat Blackjack Lanza (DQ)
Butcher Vachon beat Billy Red Cloud
The Big K beat George Gadaski

how important wrestling was to me. We had a blast watching Haystack Calhoun, Larry "the Axe" Hennig, the Big K, and other stars on the card. Two weeks later, my grandpa died of a heart attack at age sixty-nine. Maybe he sensed he didn't have much time left, but that's something I'll never know. I treasure that time we had together, and I'll never forget what he did for me.

The opening match featured the Big K versus George Gadaski. Along with Kenny "the Sodbuster" Jay, Gadaski was probably the most famous AWA job man at the time. A good athlete, Gadaski was a Canadian hockey player and a dedicated weightlifter who could bench press over five hundred pounds. He got into professional wrestling for something to do on the side, catching the attention of Gagne and Karbo in 1967. Gagne and Karbo liked Gadaski and gave him a shot doing some television matches. Billed as George "Scrap Iron" Gadaski from Great Falls, Montana, Gadaski became a valuable asset to the AWA. Gagne even put him in charge of transporting the ring and setting it up at house shows. Gadaski estimated that he was on the road two hundred days a year and logged about one hundred thousand miles taking the ring from show to show around the country.

Chapter 2

In 1971, the year my grandpa took me to the Milwaukee Auditorium to watch pro wrestling for the first time, I graduated from middle school at St. Margaret Mary in Milwaukee. I started high school at Pius XI in the fall. During my freshman year of high school, I met Mike Gutierrez while trying out for one of the school sports teams. Gutierrez also liked pro wrestling, and we became friends. Gutierrez and I made plans to see a match at the Milwaukee Arena, so we caught the bus and rode downtown to Trophy Athletic Supply. At the time, Trophy Athletic Supply was the local outlet for wrestling tickets. The only other place to get them was at the Milwaukee Arena box office. Gutierrez and I ran back and forth between the two places and checked to see which place had the better tickets. A ticket was three, four, or five dollars, depending on where you sat. We figured out pretty quickly that if we got to the ticket place early and paid five dollars, we could always get ringside seats.

On October 9, 1971, the Crusher wrestled Nick Bockwinkel. I was there to see it, sitting third row ringside on the center aisle. I also saw something else that night. Bockwinkel was getting his heat on the Crusher when a guy right behind me got out of his seat and vaulted the waist-high barricade surrounding the ring. He began crawling onto the canvas, at which point a security guard grabbed his ankle and held him until the other officers could restrain him. They marched the guy down the aisle and out of the building.

Nick Bockwinkel enjoyed a long and successful career as one of pro wrestling's greatest heels. He was famous for his articulate, thoughtful interviews in which he enraged fans by bashing his opponents using four-, five-, and six-syllable words. Bockwinkel was the son of wrestler Warren Bockwinkel, who trained him after a knee injury ended his football career at the University of Oklahoma in 1953. In addition to learning from his father, Bockwinkel studied with the legendary Lou Thesz, who schooled him to become a master of classic ring moves.

One of Bockwinkel's first pro wrestling matches was against Thesz, followed by a title match with National Wrestling Association (NWA) champion Dory Funk Jr. While gaining fame as a wrestler, Bockwinkel appeared on the television shows *Hollywood Squares, Hawaii Five-o,* and *The Monkees.* In 1970, Bockwinkel accepted an offer from Verne Gagne to work for the AWA. He was paired with another heel, Ray "the Crippler" Stevens, and managed by Bobby "the Brain" Heenan. Bockwinkel and Stevens had long, enormously popular feuds with the Crusher, Dick the Bruiser, Billy Robinson, Verne Gagne, and the team of Greg Gagne and Jim Brunzell. As a solo wrestler, he feuded with Tito Santana, Mad Dog Vachon, Otto Wanz, Jerry "the King" Lawler, Bob Backlund, Ric Flair, Stan Hansen, and Hulk Hogan.

One of the great character turns in wrestling history occurred when Verne Gagne made Bockwinkel go from a heel to a babyface during a televised match between Larry Zybszko and Greg Gagne. Using a pair of nunchucks, Zybszko viciously attacked Gagne. Suddenly, Nick Bockwinkel, Zbyszko's occasional tag team partner, jumped into the ring to save Gagne from further injury. Zbyszko responded by kayoing Bockwinkel with the gimmick, rendering him unconscious. Wrestling fans forgive and forget faster than any other group in society, and overnight Bockwinkel became a hugely popular babyface. Fans who hated him the day before now loved him.

Beginning in 1987, Bockwinkel reduced his appearances as a wrestler, instead utilizing his skills in front of the microphone to become a commentator for the World Wrestling Federation (WWF) and for World Championship Wrestling (WCW). In 1994, the WCW named him one of its commissioners and reunited him with his old manager, Bobby Heenan. Bockwinkel died in 2015 in Las Vegas.

A few years later, in April 1973, I got a job at Barnaby's Family Inn, a pizza parlor located at Eighty-Fifth Street and Capitol Drive in Milwaukee. I started as a pearl diver (restaurant slang for dishwasher), and that suited me fine. The machine that washed the dishes was a huge, chain-driven thing that operated in the manner of a car wash. I loaded dishes in a heavy-duty plastic rack, then shoved the rack forward until a claw on the drive caught the rack and dragged it through a wash and rinse cycle. It was hot and noisy, and nobody ever bothered me back there, so I figured it would be okay to fix things so as not to miss my favorite television show.

**OCTOBER 9, 1971, MILWAUKEE ARENA—
MILWAUKEE, WISCONSIN**

Ivan Koloff won a twelve-man battle royal
The Crusher beat Nick Bockwinkel (DQ)
Billy Robinson drew Ray Stevens
Blackjack Lanza drew Sailor Art Thomas
Ivan Koloff beat Billy Red Cloud
Bull Bullinski beat Jack Bence

An ad for Barnaby's Family Inn on Capitol Drive in Milwaukee.
I loved working there.

I got a little black-and-white TV for twenty-five dollars and brought it to the restaurant. I found a spot where it wouldn't get splashed, positioning the TV on top of a milk crate so I could see it from wherever I was working. On Saturday afternoons and Sunday mornings, I took care of the dirty dishes and watched wrestling at the same time! I even kept a pitcher of ice and root beer nearby, because getting paid to watch wrestling was hot, hard work. The guys I worked with loved my setup. No one ever complained about it, probably because I was the most efficient, cheerful dishwasher in Barnaby's history. One of the cooks, Bill Burczyk, said I used to imitate all the wrestling moves I saw on TV. Apparently, whenever Burczyk came by, I'd jump out from behind the dishwasher and put him in a headlock. Burczyk and I are still great friends, so there must be some truth in what he says.

One day Jim Stein, the manager at Barnaby's, called me into his office to tell me they just hired a guy named Curt who had to wear two big hearing aids powered by a battery pack that he wore on his belt. Curt was also working to improve a speech impediment caused by years of not hearing correctly. Stein warned me not to give Curt any trouble and to cut him some slack. I said, "Of course. I wouldn't be mean to the guy or anything." When I asked why I was the only one getting the lecture, Stein said, "Because you're the biggest instigator of shit around here."

I'm not sure that's entirely true. Burczyk pulled a lot of stuff. So did Larry Widen, who also worked at Barnaby's. One day, however, I started doing the dishes and the machine wouldn't turn on. I spent half an hour trying to figure out what was wrong with it before noticing that the master electrical switch leading to the machine was in the off position. I flipped it on, and the machine fired right up, so I didn't think anything more about it. Later, Burczyk walked in the kitchen with a big smirk on his face and said, "Hey, how's the dishwasher?" Then I knew he was the guy who turned it off. I grabbed the spray hose and let Burczyk have it. Just as I did, Curt came around the corner. The water hit him in the face and soaked his shirt, shorting out his battery pack and one of his hearing aids. I helped Curt dry out his pack, got the hearing aid working, then ran into Stein's office and swore on my life that the whole thing was an accident and that the water was meant to hit Burczyk. Stein just raised one eyebrow and went back to whatever he was working on. I don't know why, but everything always happened to me!

The following summer, Verne Gagne staged a battle royal at the Milwaukee Arena. It featured Harold "Oddjob" Sakata, Superstar Billy Graham, the Crusher, Baron von Raschke, and a bunch of other guys in the ring together. Burczyk, Widen, and some of the others from Barnaby's went with me to see it, and we had a blast.

After the battle royal, we went back to Barnaby's and had our own wrestling match on the lawn in front of the restaurant. I guess we got a little too enthusiastic, because one of the customers

JUNE 15, 1974, MILWAUKEE ARENA— MILWAUKEE, WISCONSIN

The Crusher and Baron von Raschke won a two-ring, twenty-four-man, $50,000 battle royal against card wrestlers and Geoff Portz, Ray Stevens, Horst Hoffman, Andre Rousimoff, Larry Heiniemi, Chris Taylor, Buddy Wolff, Billy Robinson, Ivan Putski, Moose Cholak, and Ken Patera

Nick Bockwinkel drew Wahoo McDaniel

Baron von Raschke beat Frank Nixon

Superstar Billy Graham beat Harold Sakata

Larry Hennig beat Bull Bullinski

Greg Gagne and Jim Brunzell beat Blackjack Lanza and Paul Perschmann

complained, and Stein told us to knock it off. We were doing the same thing at Widen's house around eleven thirty one night, hitting each other with dropkicks, forearm smashes, spinning toeholds, Irish whiplashes, and every other move we'd seen at the Milwaukee Arena shows. All of a sudden, a cop car pulled up with

Born in Omaha, Nebraska, in 1940, Jim Raschke was a polite, mild-mannered high school wrestler and football player who grew up to be a legend of professional wrestling. This gentleman held his larger-than-life personality in check until he appeared in the ring as Baron von Raschke, the goose-stepping Nazi known for applying the deadly claw hold to defeat his opponents. But even his ferocious ring persona took a back seat to his unforgettable weekly television interviews with Marty O'Neill and Gene Okerlund. The Baron often lapsed into incoherent rants about what he would do to his next opponents and ended with his signature closer, "Dat is all da people need to know."

After a successful amateur wrestling career and a stint in the army, Raschke joined Verne Gagne's AWA in 1966. In his first few matches, however, Raschke failed to ignite audiences at the house shows. Gagne told him he needed more training and reduced Raschke to refereeing in the meantime. Mad Dog Vachon took Raschke under his wing and tag-teamed with him at matches in Montréal. The two of them came up with the Nazi gimmick and the name Baron von Raschke before approaching Dick the Bruiser for a chance to work in Indianapolis. Bobby "the Brain" Heenan became his manager and steered Raschke into a title match against Dick the Bruiser in March 1970. The crowds went wild for Raschke as a German heel, and he played the part for all it was worth. The claw hold was immediately imitated by every schoolboy who saw it applied! The Baron and the Bruiser continued their feud in Chicago, St. Louis, and Detroit before bringing it back to Indianapolis

the siren wailing and lights flashing. The officers were responding to a call from one of the neighbors about a brawl going on outside their windows. When we explained what was going on, they laughed and told us to keep it down for the rest of the night.

In February 1975, my mom heard that a telemarketing company

for a spectacular steel cage match. Raschke spent the early 1970s working at the top of the card against other big draws such as Sailor Art Thomas, Billy Red Cloud, Ernie Ladd, and Cowboy Bob Ellis. One of Raschke's career high points during this time was wrestling Bruno Sammartino for the World Wide Wrestling Federation (WWWF) Heavyweight Championship at Madison Square Garden in New York City.

In 1974, Baron von Raschke returned to the AWA and teamed up with European star wrestler Horst Hoffman for a hugely popular series of matches against Dusty Rhodes and Superstar Billy Graham. Raschke departed the AWA in 1977 for the East Coast circuits where he feuded with Ricky Steamboat, Paul Jones, Paul Orndorff, Jimmy "Superfly" Snuka, and Jay Youngblood. In 1981, the Baron returned to the AWA when his old AWA friend, Mad Dog Vachon, was severely injured by Big John Studd and "Crusher" Jerry Blackwell. Later, Sheik Adnan Al-Kaissie came to help Blackwell, and the Crusher joined with the Baron and Mad Dog in an all-out war that AWA fans loved. When Studd and the Sheik left Blackwell, Ken Patera came on board. In March 1984, the Baron and the Crusher won the AWA Tag Team Championship from Blackwell and Patera before a sellout crowd in Green Bay, Wisconsin.

Baron von Raschke began scaling back his wrestling appearances by 1995. Together with his son, Karl, Raschke has been spending his retirement working on a film about his life and operating several business investments.

was hiring enthusiastic, bright young people to make sales over the phone. She managed to get job interviews for Widen and me, telling me, "Don't screw this up!" One Saturday morning, Widen and I reported to the telemarketing headquarters at an office building on East Mason Street. The boss's name was Frankie O'Monahanie. He told us about the job. The Milwaukee Police Brotherhood was holding a fundraising event with a couple of country western stars at the Red Carpet Expo Center, and they needed people to sell tickets over the phone. O'Monahanie gave us a scripted pitch containing information we could use to close sales. Then he handed us some pages torn out of the phone book and told us to get busy. Widen looked at me and said, "Does this mean we got the job?"

We did all right. During our first morning, the calls went something like this:

CUSTOMER: Hello?

CHRIS: Hi, my name is Chris, and I'm selling tickets to a country western show to benefit the Milwaukee Police Brotherhood.

CUSTOMER: What?

CHRIS: Yes, it's a great show for the whole family, starring Tommy Cash and Redd Stewart and . . .

CUSTOMER: (excitedly): Johnny Cash, you say?

CHRIS: Uh, no, that's Tommy Cash, his brother, I believe. And Redd Stewart . . .

CUSTOMER: (excitedly): Rod Stewart?

CHRIS: Uh, no, not Rod Stewart. That's Redd Stewart, no relation. And Tommy Cash. And Pee Wee King!

CUSTOMER: Who the hell is Pee Wee King?

CHRIS: He's part of the big country western show to benefit the Milwaukee Police Brotherhood. Tickets are just eight

dollars for the whole family or six dollars and fifty cents for
two people. How many can I count on you for?

CUSTOMER: Who's on that show again?

You get the idea. It was grueling work. Not like digging ditches
or breaking rocks, but grueling in the sense that our brains got
bashed in a little more after each encounter with a potential customer. We could extol the virtues of Pee Wee King and Tommy
Cash so many times before going off the deep end. I think Widen
and I averaged one sale for every ten attempts the first week. Then
our track record really started to go south.

I honestly don't remember who instigated the first bit of mis-
chief. But, since this is my book, let's say it was Widen. I dialed
a number and went into my sales patter. When I got to the part
about who was on the show, Widen whispered to me, "What do
you think Mr. O'Monahanie looks like in a Speedo?" I busted
out laughing and hung up the phone. After I stopped snickering,
I realized Widen might have cost me a sale. Now I was out for
revenge. Being a wrestling aficionado, I thought of a great way to
get back at him. The next time Widen began a call, I waited until
he had almost finished his pitch, then I pretended to get on a call
of my own. Holding the receiver button down with my finger, I
said, "Hello? Mrs. Vachon? May I speak to the Mad Dog?" This
time Widen had to hang up, and we both laughed uproariously
at this sophisticated bit of humor. For the next hour, it went back
and forth. "Hello, Mrs. X? Is the Doctor in?" "Hello, Mrs. von
Raschke? May I speak to the Clawmaster?" Real high-brow, sophisticated stuff.

Widen and I were actually starting to enjoy the job. We had
only one problem—our sales were in the tank. Most people
would have buckled down and tried to do something about that.
Not us. One day, we got off the bus on Wisconsin Avenue and

saw that the Center Theatre was showing a double feature horror program, *The House on Skull Mountain* and *The Legend of Hell House*. I don't remember whose idea it was to call in sick and go to the movies, but, again, let's say it was Widen's. I do admit that I made the call from a pay phone inside the lobby. When Mr. O'Monahanie answered, I said, "Hi, number twenty-six and number thirty-four are sick today. We can't come in," and hung up. I told Widen he didn't have to call in, because I took care of it for both of us and saved a dime in the process. It's a good thing we had fun at the movies, because next time we showed up for work, Mr. O'Monahanie called us into his office and said he'd been listening to some tapes of our calls. Well, that was the end of that. I can't say either one of us was all that surprised. Neither was my mom. All she said was, "I knew you'd screw it up."

That June, I graduated from Pius XI. When I did, I was faced with getting a real job or going to school. I had already thought more than once about getting into the wrestling business, but I didn't really know how to go about it. Plus, I was at least forty pounds lighter than most of the guys on TV. But I loved the theatrics and the huge personalities of wrestlers like Bobby Heenan. As I've said, Heenan was one reason why I got into wrestling. He was my first role model, and I patterned a lot of my early moves after things I'd seen him do. Still, I wasn't in great physical shape right out of high school. I was six foot one and 225 pounds, having gained some weight after a year playing high school football and lifting weights. I thought about other ways I could stay involved with wrestling, and both Widen and Burczyk suggested photography.

The three of us had gotten cameras a year earlier so we could take pictures at the matches. We had so much fun that it led us to build a little darkroom where we could make our own black-and-white prints. It seemed natural for someone who loved wrestling as much as I did to become a professional ring photographer.

After checking out some options, I learned that the Milwaukee Area Technical College (MATC)'s two-year photography program had a good reputation. I applied and was accepted in September 1976. While at MATC, I started getting myself into better shape with a weightlifting regimen at the school's gym. To earn extra cash, I also did third-shift security work at Children's Hospital of Wisconsin, so it helped that I was bulking up.

Meanwhile, I kept going with Burczyk and Widen to watch wrestling in downtown Milwaukee. One night, the Crusher was wrestling "Luscious" Johnny Valiant, and during the finish they collided with the referee and everyone was knocked unconscious. "Handsome" Jimmy Valiant, who was outside the ring acting as his brother's second, rolled Johnny out and jumped in to take his place. It was hard to tell the difference between them because both wrestlers had bleached blond mullets and wore the same color trunks. The referee came to just as Jimmy pinned the Crusher, and Johnny was declared the winner. The outcome really upset a fan, who ran up to ringside and threw a box of popcorn at the Valiants. He was escorted out of the building immediately.

In March 1978, some fellow photography students from MATC went with me to the Milwaukee Arena where the Milwaukee Sentinel Sports Show was in full swing. In the main hall, there was an advertisement looking for people to wrestle a bear. The show was run by Tuffy Truesdale, a former wrestler.

OCTOBER 25, 1975, MILWAUKEE AUDITORIUM—
MILWAUKEE, WISCONSIN

Verne Gagne beat Kim Duk
Johnny Valiant beat the Crusher
Greg Gagne and Jim Brunzell beat Bobby Heenan and
    Jimmy Valiant

Truesdale was traveling the sports show circuit with a huge black bear named Victor. Believe it or not, this was not the same Victor who had wrestled Dr. X in 1967, but Truesdale was the guy who managed both bears. My friends all said I had to try this, and I agreed, so I met with Truesdale and his people. They had me take some tests to ensure I was in decent physical condition. Then I had to sign some waivers stating I was doing this of my own free will. I passed the tests and agreed that I couldn't sue Truesdale if I got hurt. I was one of six guys picked to wrestle Victor, and I was told to come back the following afternoon.

The whole gang from MATC brought their cameras to the sports show on Sunday. I think a couple of the instructors even showed up. At the bear cage, I had to go over all the legal agreements once more just to satisfy everyone that I hadn't changed my mind. Then Truesdale came over and reminded me that actual wrestling was fine, but there was to be no punching, kicking,

Taking pictures during spring break in Jamaica.
LARRY WIDEN

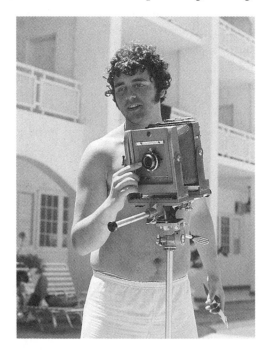

pulling Victor's fur, or trying to provoke him by going for the eyes. Why would anyone do that stuff to a six-hundred-pound animal? Even though Victor wore a muzzle, he was incredibly strong and capable of breaking a person in half.

That Sunday afternoon, almost six thousand people showed up to watch the six of us take a shot at pinning Victor. Each contestant had three minutes to do it. I was scheduled to go fourth. While I was waiting for the event to start, I thought, "There's a couple ways this could work. I could put on a good show for the crowd and have fun, or I could really try to win this thing." While I was mulling it over, they called the first guy up to the mat. Victor flattened him in less than ten seconds.

The next guy was a karate instructor, but that didn't help him. He lasted longer than the first guy, but not by much. I watched the first two wrestlers and immediately noticed why Victor had the advantage. Because of the bear's overwhelming strength, a wrestler who locked up with him in a standing position didn't have a chance. I figured the way to beat Victor was to get him off his feet and work him on the mat. I made the decision right then and there not to put on a show but to try to win. As it got closer to my time, I was sweating bullets, an absolute nervous wreck. Then they called my name and it was game on! I locked arms with Victor, but right away I dropped to my knees and grabbed his hind legs. This knocked him off balance and I was able to grab his midsection and roll him on his back. I could hear the crowd screaming as I held Victor on his back with my right arm on his left and lying on his legs so he couldn't kick out and roll out of the pin. The crowd was on their feet as the referee counted Victor out.

Truesdale contested the decision. He said I didn't really pin Victor because I didn't have both of his shoulders completely on the mat. I knew that was bullshit, and the crowd knew it too. They responded by booing and stamping their feet. Truesdale whined and complained and finally prevailed on a technicality, which is that a bear's shoulders are sloped and it's virtually impossible to get both shoulders completely on the mat at the same time. Still, whether or not Victor's shoulders were on the mat, I had that bear immobilized. That fact is that Truesdale didn't want word getting around that somebody had actually beaten Victor.

Twice I wrestled another bear that summer, this time at the Brookfield Square shopping center. The referee declared the first

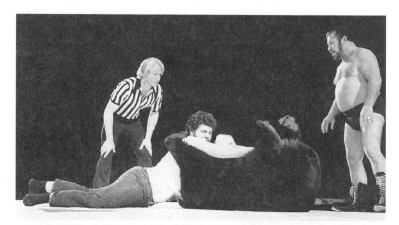

Wrestling Victor, a six-hundred-pound black bear, at the Milwaukee Sentinel Sports Show in 1978. LARRY WIDEN

match a draw. When I went back the next day, I made some mis-
calculations that gave the bear a momentary advantage and it cost
me. The bear caught me by the shoulder and partially tore my
rotator cuff. That tear eventually healed, but it gave me problems
for years afterward. Sometimes when I was in the ring, I'd signal
my opponent to lay off my shoulder and put me in a headlock
because my shoulder would be in such agony.

Later that year, I was reading the sports section and noticed an
ad for a "Superstars of Wrestling" show at Jefferson Hall. I went
down there with the idea of showing the promoter some of my
pictures, hoping to get on as the official photographer for the event.
I met "King Kong" Al Patterson, owner of the United Wrestling Association (UWA). Patterson said he couldn't afford a photographer,
but after he sized me up, he asked me if I wanted to be the manager
that night for Fred "the Enforcer" Torres. I said I did, and I assured
Patterson that I knew exactly what to do. I had seen Bobby Heenan
do it on TV a million times. On September 10, 1978, I finally got
into a pro wrestling ring. I took a couple of bumps, and the crowd
loved it! More important, Patterson gave me a spot on his next card.
After the match, I couldn't wait to go back. I even added extra time
to my workout routine by lifting weights with some of Patterson's
wrestlers at the Martin Luther King Jr. Center.

**SEPTEMBER 10, 1978, JEFFERSON HALL—
MILWAUKEE, WISCONSIN**

Wild Bill Bradley and Mike Scarbelli vs. Indian Pete and
    Aurilio Rodriguez
Tom Pall vs. Al Patterson
Black Shadow vs. Angel Rivera
Fred Torres vs. Bad Brains Lucas—Chris Curtis, manager
Doctor Killer vs. Kirk the Lumberjack

Jefferson Hall, at 2617 West Fond du Lac Avenue, was orignally built in 1928 as the Freie Gemeinde (Free Congregational) Society Clubhouse. The attractive two-story structure was done in the popular Federal Revival style with red brick and limestone trim. At that time, the neighborhood surrounding the clubhouse was heavily populated by German families. Just down the street was the Kino, Milwaukee's only German motion picture theater.

Freedom Hall, as it was referred to in English, housed a gymnasium, eight bowling alleys, two bars, and an auditorium for dinners, dances, and other entertainment. Two thousand people could be seated in the auditorium for presentations, and attorney Clarence Darrow and social activist Margaret Sanger were two notable personalities who spoke there. In 1940, the local architectural firm of Grassold & Johnson completed plans for a $20,000 addition to the east side of the building that included a larger ballroom for live music and stage shows. As soldiers returned from World War II, low-interest government loans made it possible for them to buy starter homes in newly developed areas of Wauwatosa and other communities west of Sixtieth Street. African American families moved into the homes near Freedom Hall, and in the 1960s, the name was changed to Jefferson Hall. At that time, the primary renters were labor unions who used the space for meetings and functions. By 1977, decline in rentals caused the owners to encourage other usage. Church services, music shows, and wrestling events were just a few of the new entertainment options offered by ambitious local businessmen like Al Patterson. In recent years, the building has housed religious organizations such as the Kingdom Missionary Baptist Church.

Patterson tried to be successful with his stable of wrestlers. He held cards at Jefferson Hall on the north side, the Crystal Palace on the south side, and at annual events such as the African World Festival. Eventually, Patterson got Verne Gagne's attention when he started running a TV show on Channel 24. It was called

Learning how to wrestle in 1978.
DENNIS MULTERER

Jefferson Hall, at Twenty-Sixth Street and Fond du Lac Avenue in Milwaukee, is where I began my wrestling career. WHI IMAGE ID 143457

Superstars of Wrestling and featured some of Gagne's jobbers such as Armando Rodriguez, Cesar Pabón, and Ben DeLeon. Independent wrestlers also appeared on *Superstars of Wrestling* from time to time. They included Bulldog Brower, Dom DeNucci, Ricky Rickowski, Jimmy Foxx, Hank Duchek, Mr. Reed, Thunderbolt Williams, Nature Boy Hanson, Rocky Brewer, Mike the Demon, Mr. Haiti, the Black Marvel, Jeff May, and the Beast. I wrestled most of them at one time or another. Yet it wasn't until Patterson rented the Milwaukee Auditorium and ran house shows with stars such as Randy "Macho Man" Savage, Ronnie Garvin, and Cowboy Bob Orton that he really pissed Gagne off. One of those cards outdrew the monthly AWA show, bringing in more than four thousand people.

Years later, Patterson ended up competing with Vince McMahon Jr.'s company, Titan Sports, over the right to use the name *Superstars of Wrestling*. By entering tapes of Patterson's TV show into evidence, Patterson's attorneys proved that the Milwaukee-based UWA used *Superstars of Wrestling* six years before McMahon did. Ultimately, Al Patterson was awarded $100,000 by the courts in 1983.

The Milwaukee Auditorium was the site of many pro wrestling bouts from the 1950s through the 1980s. WHI IMAGE ID 47409

Chapter 3

Anthony Hopkins has a great spot in the movie *Zorro* where he tells Zorro, played by Antonio Banderas, "When the pupil is ready, the master will appear." That's exactly what happened to me when I met Steve Hall at Jeff Jakubiak's wrestling training facility at Federation Hall. Steve's dad was Red Hall, a longtime Milwaukee disc jockey who did the ring announcements at the Milwaukee Arena wrestling shows. Through his father's connections, Hall had gotten into the business as a job man working as Tom "Rocky" Stone. In addition, Hall was training and developing job men with the skills needed for taping *All-Star Wrestling* in Minneapolis. Hall's regular crew included Frank Hill, Vito Martino, Armando Rodriguez, Cesar Pabón, Peter Lee, and Bob Amel. Most of all, Hall taught me how to be a better wrestler. He taught me how to go over the top rope and hit the concrete floor without getting hurt, along with new holds and moves. Thankfully, Hall also showed me how to pace myself so I could go ten or even twelve minutes in the ring without running out of gas. That was a lifesaver on more than one occasion.

Hall also taught wrestlers how to perform for an audience. He stressed the importance of being able to read a crowd and how to work their emotions with your ring personality. Developing a persona started with the decision to be a babyface or a heel. If you're a babyface, or a face, such as Greg Gagne or Jim Brunzell, you smile, wave, follow the rules, and be nice. If you're the heel, you needle the crowd, cheat, and beg for mercy when your

Wrestling Steve Hall, the guy who trained me to be a job man. LARRY WIDEN

opponent finally starts his comeback. Well, I didn't have to think long about which I wanted to be. I always loved the heels such as Bockwinkel and Ray "the Crippler" Stevens, Bobby "the Brain" Heenan, and Mad Dog Vachon. I could emulate them perfectly.

Ultimately, Hall made me a better job man, and his counsel was invaluable. Learning under him was the next best thing to attending Verne Gagne's pro wrestling camp in Minnesota. Gagne's six-month camp was very tough. Students worked hard for eight hours a day, six days a week. I've been told it was similar to Navy SEAL or Special Forces training. Consequently, the students who made it through usually became headline wrestlers. Graduates of Gagne's camp include Ric Flair, Bob Remus (Super Destroyer II and later Sgt. Slaughter), Greg Gagne, Jim Brunzell, Buck Zumhofe, Chris Taylor, Ken Patera, and Khosrow Vaziri (the Iron Sheik), to name just a few.

On December 5, 1978, I wrestled in my first match at Federation Hall. I wore a mask and wrestled as the Skull. My opponent was Bad Brains Lucas. Lucas hailed from Puerto Rico but lived just a few blocks from Federation Hall. He was good, but that night Lucas insisted on doing a blade job before he was ready and cut his forehead pretty badly, which led to his bleeding uncontrollably all over the ring. In those days, we didn't really worry about blood-borne diseases. It's a good thing we didn't because blood was everywhere. Today I don't think that would fly. After the match with Lucas, I worked with Fred Torres as a tag team. He was the Enforcer I and I was the Enforcer II.

Not long afterward, Hall said to me, "You're ready for TV." Hall took me and a few others to St. Paul to appear on *All-Star Wrestling*. That was a big moment for me. In the business of professional wrestling, there are two career benchmarks. The first is to become skilled enough to land a television spot. The second is to get booked for a house show at an arena or an auditorium. I felt like a million bucks when I was invited to appear on *All-Star*

Applying the deadly cobra clutch at the Milwaukee Area Technical College photography studio. LARRY WIDEN

Wrestling at Federation Hall as Enforcer II. DENNIS MULTERER

Wrestling after just eight weeks on the job! Some guys wrestle for years and never get so far.

When we arrived at the TV station in St. Paul, I went upstairs to the dressing room and sat down. As the main eventers began walking in, I felt like I was in Hollywood. There I was, a twenty-two-year-old wrestling fan suddenly hanging out with the guys I'd been watching since 1966! As I got to know them, it seemed like the heels—the wrestlers who were the nastiest on TV and in the arenas—turned out to be the nicest guys in person. Conversely, the babyfaces—who seemed so nice and friendly on TV—were the biggest jerks. My first TV outing was a tag team match against Greg Gagne and Jim Brunzell. They called themselves the High Flyers and were one of the biggest draws in the business at the time. In the second fall, Brunzell beat me with a figure-four leg-lock, and the match ended there. I got paid eighty-five dollars, and I couldn't have been more thrilled. We cashed our checks at

At the Milwaukee
Area Technical Col-
lege photography
studio. LARRY WIDEN

a liquor store near the TV station, then all of us from Milwaukee
had a big buffet dinner before driving six hours home.

It wasn't long before I was going to the Twin Cities to shoot
television matches twice a month, which I did for the next ten
years. Verne Gagne liked me from the start, which was good because no one ever got a second chance with him. If you screwed
up, you were out. Gagne would tell his business partner Wally
Karbo, who did the actual bookings for the matches, to tell Steve

Working with Greg
Gagne. I worked
Greg Gagne more
times than any
other wrestler. He
weighed only 210
pounds, but he
was strong enough
to body slam a
three-hundred-
pound opponent.
GREG GAGNE

Hall not to bring so-and-so back again. Then Hall would have to find someone else.

You never knew what was going to happen around Gagne, especially when he lost his temper. One time, when Hall was out of town, Dick Reynolds was responsible for bringing in the jobbers for TV. Reynolds was actually Dick Raniewicz, a Milwaukee-area high school math teacher who wrestled on the side. Verne had promised Reynolds a lot of work in the summers when Reynolds was free from teaching classes, but it didn't work out that way. Gagne ended up giving most of what he had promised to Reynolds to a guy named Doug Gilbert. After that, Reynolds left the business because the commutes became too much for him during the school year. In any event, Reynolds brought in Herman "the German" Schaefer and two other out-of-shape guys named Dallas Young and David Starr. In the dressing room, Gagne took one look at the build on Young and went ballistic. Gagne got right in his face and yelled, "You fat bitch! Who brought you up here?" He went on a rant about Young having no muscles, and then he turned to Starr and said, "How much can you bench?" Starr answered, "About seventy-five pounds." Gagne said, "Goddamn it, my daughter can lift more than that." Now he was really mad. With Young and Starr trying to diffuse the situation, Gagne screamed, "Get the fuck out of here and don't come back." Then he yelled at Reynolds and said, "Don't ever bring guys like that up here again!"

Karbo loved booking Schaefer for Minneapolis TV because Schaefer was a huge guy who looked like the Frankenstein monster without the makeup. I was supposed to wrestle him and another wrestler, Woody Wilson, in Milwaukee. Wilson had his heart set on making some stupid special outfit for the match because Schaefer usually wore a floor-length cape his wife had made out of the lime green curtains that once hung in their living room windows. At the last minute, though, Schaefer had the brilliant idea for him and Wilson to wear matching polka dot shirts. Wilson weighed about 290 pounds at the time, and Schaefer was bigger at 320. Just imagine what two guys that size in polka dots looked like. I thought Wilson was gonna cry when Schaefer made him wear that shirt!

Whenever Schaefer did television for the AWA, it seemed like he was booked in matches against Jim Brunzell. Brunzell probably thought the office was punishing him for something. I usually got to wrestle Greg Gagne. I think the office matched us up that way simply because Gagne and Brunzell handled us well. One thing's for certain, though: Schaefer was not exactly a joy to travel with. He had a horrible diet. Most of us didn't eat well on the road, but Schaefer took it to another level. He thought nothing of spending the six-hour drive from Milwaukee to Minneapolis eating pickled herring, Slim Jims, pickles, and cheese while downing bottle after bottle of beer. When he finally finished eating, he'd light up one of his cheap, stinky cigars. What a mess. Because of this, Schaefer was often the butt of our jokes. For instance, at a house show in Rockford, Illinois, the Iron Sheik managed to catch a bat and hide it in Schaefer's duffle bag. When Schaefer pulled his wrestling gear out, the bat flew right in his face and freaked him out.

Wrestling wasn't all fun and exciting. There were times when I had to deal with things that I hadn't experienced before. One that comes to mind happened in July 1979, when I was matched against the British wrestler Billy Robinson. I was a little nervous because I hadn't wrestled Robinson before. Worse, he had a reputation of being tough on the newer guys. I was on friendly footing with Bockwinkel, so I asked him how to handle Robinson. Bockwinkel said, "Yeah, Billy can be rough, but the best thing to do is just listen to him, do what he says and you'll be fine." That sounded pretty good to me. Taking Nick's advice, I went up to Robinson, introduced myself, and asked him to outline the angle. Robinson went over the moves and told me how we would finish.

When we got in the ring, I followed his lead and we locked up. Then I got him in the corner and made like I was gonna throw a punch at his face. He glared at me and growled an obscenity. I was stunned, and didn't know what to do. This wasn't part of what we had gone over in the dressing room. I held the punch and Robinson maneuvered me into a double suplex. It hurt like hell, so I knew Robinson was stretching me, intentionally trying to hurt me using a painful submission hold. He bent me backward in the move known as the Boston crab, which can easily result in a broken back. I submitted right away to end the match. When it was over, I didn't know what had gone wrong in the ring with Robinson, but I was positive I didn't want any more crap from him in the dressing room. I thought, "I'm done. I don't need to be treated like this." On the way out, I saw Wally Karbo and asked him if I had done something wrong. Karbo just blew me off, saying "Don't worry about it." Bockwinkel and Ray Stevens came over to me, and Stevens said, "Do not quit over this. It was nothing. It's just how Billy gets." Bockwinkel added, "We all know you're good at this and you're doing a great job." I'm grateful to Bockwinkel and Stevens for their support, and believe me when I say it came at a time when I really needed it. Stevens told me that Robinson liked to be tough on the new guys primarily to see if they had what it takes. "And you got through it," Bockwinkel said, "so congratulations."

Others didn't take Robinson's abuse the way I had. Once his reputation for hazing new wrestlers with submission tactics got out, guys took action. When Superstar Billy Graham came to the AWA, he went right up to Robinson before their match and told him he was bringing a razor blade into the ring, and at the first hint of any shit, he was going to cut Robinson to ribbons. That's a true story. Graham never got the chance to wrestle Robinson that night. Somebody must have tipped Verne Gagne off to what was up, because Gagne canceled their match on the spot. Gagne was tough, and he usually looked the other way if Robinson bullied

One of Britain's most decorated wrestlers, Billy Robinson was born in Manchester, England, in 1939 into a family of bareknuckle boxing champs. At age four, Robinson began boxing until the age of eleven when an eye injury ended any chance of his being licensed to box in England. He began wrestling at sixteen, the legal age to compete. Robinson's father sent him to study with legendary wrestling trainer Billy Riley at The Snake Pit, one of the toughest wrestling schools in the world. Riley taught Robinson the famously brutal Lancashire wrestling style, in which any throw or hold was considered fair game. As a result, Robinson became a master of catch wrestling, in which a wrestler delivers increasing anatomical pain to his opponent until a submission ends the match.

When the 190-pound Robinson faced a 350-pound wrestler from the Lebanese Olympic team, Robinson broke his opponent's leg within thirty seconds. He admitted feeling bad about it but defended his actions by stating the other wrestler had failed to tap out. By this time, Robinson had acquired a reputation for violence in the ring, and a number of wrestlers refused to work with him. After winning several light heavyweight British and European championships, Robinson relocated to America and began working for Verne Gagne in 1970. His matches included feuds with Abdullah the Butcher, the Masked Destroyer, Ken Patera, Angelo Mosca, Paul Ellering, and Rick Martel. Robinson often teamed with the Crusher for matches against Nick Bockwinkel and Ray "the Crippler" Stevens.

Although Robinson enjoyed the entertainment aspect of pro wrestling, his heart was in teaching other wrestlers to become shooters using the submission techniques of catch wrestling. Robinson was idolized in Japan for his catch skills, and he schooled many mixed martial artists and jiu-jitsu experts in his style. Robinson operated an acclaimed wrestling school in Arkansas for a number of years before his death in 2014.

the new guys. But Graham didn't leave any room for working it out in the ring, and Gagne was too savvy a businessman to have one or both of his big attractions unable to perform at a house show.

On the other side of the spectrum from Billy Robinson was a guy like the Crusher. On one of my flights out of Minneapolis,

---

MARCH 18, 1979, MINNEAPOLIS TV, AND MARCH 31, 1979, DAVENPORT TV

Greg Gagne and Jim Brunzell beat Tom Stone and Chris Curtis
Nick Bockwinkel beat Dick Reynolds
The Crusher beat Fernando Torres
Jesse Ventura beat Ted Wicker
Billy Robinson beat Kenny Jay

APRIL 1, 1979, MINNEAPOLIS TV, AND APRIL 14, 1979, DAVENPORT TV

Steve Olsonoski and Paul Ellering beat Ted Wicker and Chris Curtis
Jesse Ventura beat Peter Lee
The Crusher beat Armando Rodriguez
Super Destroyer Mark II beat Kenny Jay
Nick Bockwinkel beat Frank Hill

MAY 6, 1979, MINNEAPOLIS TV

Steve Olsonoski and Paul Ellering beat Doug Somers and Chris Curtis
Dick Reynolds beat Jesse Ventura (DQ)
Doug Gilbert beat Peter Lee
Nick Bockwinkel beat Tom Stone
Bobby Duncum beat George Gadaski

I noticed he loved martinis almost as much as beer. We talked all the way back to Milwaukee while enjoying a couple of those James Bond specials. You know, shaken not stirred and with a twist of lemon instead of an olive. "Whaddya tink a dat mug Hoiman?" the Crusher asked me. I knew he was referring to Herman Schaefer. "Well," I started to say, "He's not too . . .," and before I could say anything else, the Crusher growled, "He can't work." That made me laugh, because with Schaefer and the Crusher in the ring, that meant there were *two* guys who couldn't work. The Crusher was a great guy with a huge personality, and he sold all his matches during the interviews. In the ring, his moves were basically the eye-poke, the headlock, and the bolo punch. To be fair, those moves suited him because the Crusher never pretended to be anything other than a brawler. All the Crusher needed was a guy like me to work him and make him look good. Outside of a few battle royals, that's something that never happened, and let me tell you, it would have been an honor to wrestle him.

The Crusher was born Reggie Lisowski in south Milwaukee in 1926. He played fullback in high school, and upon graduation in 1944, he joined the army. Eventually, the army shipped him out to Germany with the Tenth Infantry. It was there that one of his instructors got him interested in wrestling and weightlifting. When Lisowski came back to Milwaukee in 1948, he began wrestling at the Eagles Club. His first pro bout was at the Paris Ballroom on November 30, 1949. The Paris held wrestling matches every Friday night. Admission was seventy-five cents for general admission and one dollar for reserved seats. Lisowski wrestled regularly at the Paris until 1952, when Fred Kohler, a promoter from Chicago, signed him to a contract. Kohler put Lisowski on his Dumont network TV show and sent him on the road to get more experience in the ring. Among the wrestlers Lisowski faced along the way were Billy Goelz, the Mighty Atlas, Hard Boiled Haggerty, Hans Schmidt, Bill Melby, and Pat O'Connor.

His match against National Wrestling Alliance (NWA) champion
Lou Thesz in September 1952 was Lisowski's first title shot. For
the first few years of his career, Lisowski was a beloved fan favorite. By 1954, his hair was bleached white-blonde and he worked
as a heel, ensuring boos from avid ringside fans. Lisowski's career
took another upward turn a few years later when he was paired
with Stan Holek, a muscular, bleached-blonde heel who could
have passed for his twin. Lisowski and Holek wrestled as the Lisowski Brothers for the first time on January 26, 1956, at the South
Side Armory in Milwaukee. They wore pink silk jackets and used
every underhanded tactic in the book. Before going their separate
ways in 1959, Lisowski and Holek took on babyface tag teams
such as Verne Gagne and Wilbur Snyder, and Dick the Bruiser
and Hans Schmidt.

Wrestling as a heel, Lisowski's first solo match was against
Gagne in Minneapolis. Then he wrestled Kenny Jay in Chicago.
Lisowski was billed as Crusher Lisowski, but in short order, that
changed to "the Crusher" or "da Crusher," depending on who was
doing the talking. Some of the Crusher's great early matches were
against Bruno Sammartino, one of the most popular wrestlers in
the history of the sport. Sammartino and his family came to the
United States from Italy after World War II and settled in Pittsburgh, Pennsylvania. He wasn't quite six feet tall, but his dedica-
tion to weight training helped him bulk up to 280 pounds. In 1959,
Sammartino benched 565 pounds, setting a new world record.
That same year, he made his pro wrestling debut and became a
fan favorite after appearing on the *Studio Wrestling* TV show. Sammartino's legendary feud with the Crusher began with a grueling
match in 1961 at the Bronx Coliseum. They met six months later
in Chicago, and three more times in Pittsburgh. At his seventieth
birthday dinner, Bruno recalled that the Crusher broke his nose
twice, and he broke the Crusher's only once!

In 1965, the Crusher switched sides and became a babyface,

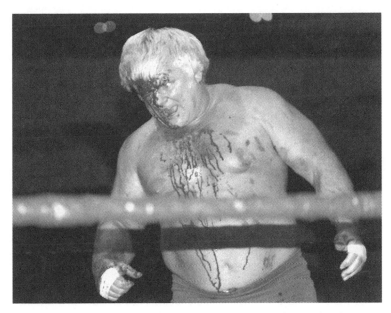

The Crusher getting down and dirty during a 1974 match in Milwaukee.
LARRY WIDEN

the persona he would keep for the remainder of his career. Fans
who once jeered and booed the Crusher were now solidly in his
corner. It was difficult not to like the Crusher. He claimed that he
trained for matches by running along the lakefront in Milwaukee
with a full barrel of beer on his shoulder. Longtime AWA announcer Rodger Kent noted that by the end of the Crusher's run,
the beer was gone. Afterward, the Crusher would dance all night
with Polish barmaids to increase his stamina. In 2019, a life-size
bronze statue of the Crusher was unveiled in South Milwaukee.
More than ten thousand people showed up to the celebration.

As I said, the Crusher's great opponent, Bruno Sammartino,
has, like the Crusher, long been considered one of the great babyfaces in the history of professional wrestling. Sammartino was
world heavyweight champion in Vince McMahon Sr.'s World
Wide Wrestling Federation (WWWF) beginning in 1963, when

he beat Buddy Rogers, until he lost the title to Ivan Koloff in 1971. He regained the championship, this time from Stan Stasiak, in 1973, and held it for four years before losing to Superstar Billy Graham in Baltimore. Wherever he went, Sammartino was a huge draw, setting box office records at Madison Square Garden when he was matched against Cowboy Bill Watts.

Wrestlers loved working Sammartino. He always took care of his opponents, doing his best to sell matches, even for the heel, especially when the heel was getting his heat. Yet, predictably, there were guys who tried to take advantage of Sammartino's generous nature in the ring. One was Dr. Bill Miller, a six foot six, three-hundred-pound giant. Before turning pro, Miller had been Big Ten heavyweight champion while wrestling for Ohio State University. Once, Miller was partnered in a tag team match with Baron Mikel Sicluna against Tony Parisi and Sammartino. Miller tried to be a shooter with Sammartino by going for his legs. He underestimated Sammartino, who caught Miller in a front face lock and choked him until he passed out. Miller was lucky, because Sammartino could have killed him with that hold.

I was lucky enough to meet Sammartino on several occasions when I eventually worked for Vince McMahon Jr.'s World Wrestling Federation (WWF). At the time, Sammartino was doing television commentary with Jesse Ventura and McMahon. He was always a gentleman, and it was fun to hang out with him.

One guy I'm glad I never worked with in the ring was Ed Farhat, professionally known as the Sheik. Farhat's persona was one of the best in the business, as the Sheik terrorized fans and even a few opponents. But Farhat was also the most prolific user of illegal foreign objects, such as pencils, forks, steel chairs, and other things that weren't allowed inside the ring. He even used magician's flash paper. When ignited, the flash paper temporarily blinded his opponents or distracted the referee. Needless to say, everyone was always on edge around the Sheik, who came to the ring accompanied by his manager, Abdullah Farouk. Farouk's real name was Ernie Roth, and he wore a Shriner fez and sunglasses as part of his costume. I always thought he looked like one of the villains in the old 1940s mummy movies.

What most people don't know about Farhat is that he paid his dues by working for many years as a job man. As the Sheik of Araby, Farhat was a familiar figure on the Midwest pro wrestling circuit. In September 1955, Farhat lost big matches to Hans Schmidt at the Milwaukee Auditorium and to Verne Gagne at the Fairgrounds Cow Palace in Fond du Lac, Wisconsin. The following year, Farhat was beaten by Dick the Bruiser at Madison's Dane County Fairgrounds Arena and again by Verne Gagne in Rockford, Illinois, and Beloit, Wisconsin. In the summer of 1956, Wilbur Snyder beat him in Milwaukee, as did Bill Melby. When WTMJ Channel 4 began televising wrestling from Milwaukee's South Side Armory in 1957, Farhat lost matches to Hans Hermann and Larry Chene.

In the 1970s and early 1980s, Farhat was regarded as the greatest professional wrestling villain of all time. Nevertheless, he damaged his career by refusing to lose matches. Eventually, the fans abandoned Farhat because they never got to see him get what the babyfaces promised.

In 1974, Farhat brought André the Giant to Toronto, selling out Maple Leaf Gardens in the process. What could have been a great match between them was ruined by Farhat's stubborn refusal to lose. When André the Giant headbutted Farhat into next week and clobbered him with his huge arms, it looked like Farhat didn't have a chance. That changed when, as the crowd roared, the Sheik threw a fireball at André the Giant while the referee was distracted. Four minutes into the match, it was over. André the Giant lost, and Farhat was still undefeated. Fans continued to turn their backs on him.

Farhat was a professional, so it's not surprising that once he became a star, he looked to the future, which in the pro wrestling business is booking the story arcs. In addition to wrestling, Farhat ran the Detroit office for twenty years starting in 1965.

Bobby Heenan is quite simply the greatest personality in the history of pro wrestling. It's unlikely his quick wit, ringside antics, hilarious on-camera interviews, and ability to invoke over-the-top negative reactions from fans will ever be surpassed.

Heenan was born in Chicago, Illinois, in 1944 and grew up in Indianapolis. He dropped out of school in eighth grade to help support his mother and grandmother. One of his favorite jobs was selling programs, refreshments, and other souvenirs at Dick the Bruiser's wrestling shows. He carried bags for the wrestlers and helped set up for the house shows. Bruiser took a liking to Heenan, and when Bobby was seventeen, Bruiser put him in the ring as "Pretty Boy" Bobby Heenan versus Calvin "Prince" Pullins. Heenan proved himself to be a very talented wrestler, but he proved himself to have even more talent furthering the various storylines that emerged during his television show interviews.

He became a manager, appearing at house shows with Angelo Poffo, Chris Markoff, the Assassins (Guy Mitchell and Joe Tomasso), the Valiant Brothers, and Blackjack Lanza. By the early 1970s, Heenan had turned Lanza into one of the most hated wrestling villains in the country. St. Louis promoter Sam Muchnick was impressed with Heenan's accomplishments and hired him to work for the St. Louis Wrestling Club. Heenan made the move because he was in a dispute with his former mentor, Dick the Bruiser, over payment for appearing in a huge wrestling event at Indianapolis's Market Square Arena.

In 1974, Verne Gagne brought Heenan to the AWA where his star continued to rise. Heenan, now known as "the Brain," famously managed the tag team of Nick Bockwinkel and Ray "the Crippler" Stevens in feuds with the Crusher and Dick the Bruiser. At the height of his popularity in the AWA, Greg Gagne brought a weasel costume into the ring and challenged Heenan to a match in which the loser would wear the suit.

Heenan was infuriated about this and clobbered Greg on the head from behind while wearing a gimmick arm cast. Verne jumped in the ring and saved the unconscious Greg. That began a popular series of weasel suit matches that drew fans in droves to arenas in Milwaukee, Green Bay, and Peoria, Illinois. Milwaukee's favorite son, the Crusher, even got into baiting Heenan with a wind-up jack-in-the-box toy that he cranked while singing "Pop Goes the Weasel" in his trademark gravelly baritone. Heenan later had a number of weasel suit matches with Buck Zumhofe.

During a 1983 match in Japan against Atsushi Onita, Heenan broke his neck. Though he recovered, the injury limited Heenan's ability to perform in the ring as he once had. He returned to Minneapolis and initiated a brawl with the Fabulous Ones during a TV interview, which resulted in promoter Wally Karbo suspending him for one year. The suspension was a graceful way for Heenan to leave the AWA.

In 1984, Heenan accepted Vince McMahon Jr.'s offer to join the New York–based WWF and manage Jesse "the Body" Ventura and Big John Studd. Within five years, Heenan also added Ken Patera, "Playboy" Buddy Rose, Paul "Mr. Wonderful" Orndorff, André the Giant, Arn Anderson, Harley Race, and "Ravishing" Rick Rude to his stable of wrestlers. His famous feud with the Ultimate Warrior led to a series of weasel suit matches that recalled his glory days with Verne Gagne and the AWA.

By 1993, recurring pain from the neck injury he had suffered a decade earlier forced Heenan to leave the ring permanently. McMahon took the opportunity to pair him up with Gorilla Monsoon, another former wrestler, to act as a ringside color commentator for televised matches. Heenan excelled in his new role, and fans tuned in just to witness the hilarious interactions that occurred when Heenan deliberately taunted Monsoon during the broadcasts. Referring to himself as a television journalist, Heenan routinely bashed the

Bobby Heenan,
left, and Nick
Bockwinkel, right,
were two huge
influences on me
when I was grow-
ing up. AMERICAN
WRESTLING
ASSOCIATION

babyface wrestlers while praising the heels. He referred to job men as "ham-and-eggers" and the fans as "humanoids." When Heenan finally retired, he and Monsoon staged an on-air fight that ended when Monsoon threw Heenan and his bags onto the street outside Madison Square Garden.

For the next ten years, Heenan worked for a number of wrestling shows and circuits in between battles with throat cancer. Treatments for cancer and the subsequent weight loss took their toll, dramatically altering both Heenan's voice and appearance. In 2009, Milwaukee Mayor Tom Barrett issued a proclamation declaring December 5 Bobby Heenan Day in the city. Heenan passed away in Florida in 2017.

Yet a particularly memorable moment in the Sheik's career came when he finally met his match in Lou Thesz. Thesz hated gimmick wrestlers with little or no amateur wrestling background. After the Sheik threw fire in Thesz's face during a match in Chicago, Thesz threatened to break the Sheik's legs. Thesz chased the Sheik out of the building, and later the cops found him hiding under a city bus across the street. In addition to his feud with Thesz, the Sheik had a long-standing feud with Bobo Brazil, the world's most popular black wrestler at the time next to Sailor Art Thomas. The feuds were a good thing for the Sheik, as nothing keeps fans buying tickets like a well-scripted grudge that plays out over the course of a year or more.

The reason I put so much emphasis on guys such as Reggie Lisowski and Ed Farhat is that they were my teachers. By emulating them, I learned a great deal about my craft in a very short amount of time. Any wrestler with a bit of athleticism and training can perform adequately inside the ring. But the real professionals, the guys who really know what they are doing, are the ones who can read the crowd on a given night and play to the energy in the air. Babyfaces can get a reaction just by twirling a finger, but the heels are the ones who sell the tickets. If the crowd is in a surly mood, the best heels pick up on that and mock the people sitting in the ringside seats to make them really mad. Nick Bockwinkel, for example, used to find an overweight guy and cruelly taunt him about his potbelly or multiple chins. Bobby Heenan would make fun of a guy's wife or girlfriend until the guy wanted to kill him. Heenan was the best at getting people in the crowd to hate him, always dancing out of the way knowing security guards would restrain any angry fans.

Pro wrestling at the height of its popularity was live theater at its finest. Whether the fans realized it or not, they were getting a hell of a lot of entertainment for the five-dollar price of admission. What we offered was Shakespeare for the blue-collar crowd, and the crowd loved it.

Chapter 4

In May 1979, I began to work for Pat O'Connor. O'Connor ran the St. Louis, Missouri, office for Central States Wrestling, having entered the business in the mid-1950s before becoming the NWA world champion in 1959. He held that title until June 30, 1961, when O'Connor lost the belt to Buddy Rogers in front of thirty-eight thousand fans at Chicago's Comiskey Park. It was three decades before that attendance record would be broken.

In September 1963, O'Connor, Harley Race, and Bob Geigel purchased the St. Louis and Kansas City territories from Sam Muchnick after Muchnick, who was a legendary wrestling promoter, announced his retirement. O'Connor handled St. Louis, Geigel handled Kansas City, and Race handled a little bit of both. By 1980, Verne Gagne had started to trade wrestling talent with Central States, myself included. Steve Hall took me and four others to Missouri where we taped three shows for KSHB Channel 41 in Kansas City, and two shows for St. Louis KPLR Channel 11. In St. Louis, we filmed at the Chase Park Plaza Hotel. The Chase was famous for its luxurious guest rooms, bars, and restaurants. It has some infamy attached to it as well. In 1953, baseball player Jackie Robinson publicly criticized the hotel's management for refusing to serve him in their restaurant, even as the other Dodger players ate there. The Chase responded by lifting the ban prohibiting service to African Americans.

The Chase began accommodating professional wrestling shows in 1959. To do so, owner Harold Koplar built a huge television studio in his hotel. The house shows, "Wrestling at the Chase," were held in the ballroom. I got seventy dollars for the Chase shows and eighty-five dollars for the Kansas City shows. In June 2017, the Chase was acquired by the Sonesta International Hotels Corporation and is now called the Chase Park Plaza Royal Sonesta Hotel.

I worked some tough guys at the Chase. One of the toughest was Gene "Big Thunder" Kiniski. Our match took place in September 1979 during three television tapings I did at the Chase. In 1961, Kiniski was the AWA world heavyweight champion as well as two-time AWA tag team champion with Hard Boiled Hagerty. Five years later, Kiniski defeated Lou Thesz to become the NWA world heavyweight champion. Kiniski was a brawler who wrestled in the style of Killer Kowalski, which is to say he beat his opponent unmercifully from start to finish.

For a jobber like me, Kiniski was tough to put over because he was old school all the way. He was a stiff in the ring who really

Gene Kiniski was an old-school brawler who nearly beat me senseless in the ring. CENTRAL STATES WRESTLING

couldn't do anything besides beat up his opponents. During the match, I got Kiniski on his back and began hitting him with working, or pulled, punches. Kiniski told me to hit him harder, so I hit him again but still pulled the punch. He got madder and said, "Goddammit, hit me!" I did as I was told. I wound up and hit Kiniski in the mouth with a closed fist as hard as I could. His eyes lit up, so I socked him again, this time right in the nose. He was bleeding profusely, and I thought, "I'm dead." I was right. Kiniski threw me on my back and beat on me until I was a mess. My face was bloody and my chest was like raw hamburger. When I went back to the dressing room, "Bruiser" Bob Sweetan innocently asked who worked me over. I told him, "Kiniski." Then Sweetan asked me how the match went. Funny stuff, now that I'm writing this.

Wrestling Pat O'Connor was a lesson in itself. O'Connor loved putting jobbers in a front face lock on TV. Then the jobber would escape the hold, and O'Connor would put him in a hammer lock or half nelson. After ten minutes, I had enough of that, so I let O'Connor roll me up for the pin.

Things didn't go so easily for O'Connor one night in Wichita, Kansas, when he was on the undercard against Ron McFarland. O'Connor showed up nursing a bad hangover. When he was in the ring with McFarland, O'Connor told McFarland to put him in a headlock and really work it. McFarland got O'Connor in the hold, and O'Connor immediately fell asleep. McFarland didn't know what to do, so he worked the headlock until O'Connor woke up, then McFarland pinned him. Only in pro wrestling!

In addition to Kiniski and O'Connor, some of my St. Louis matches included bouts against "Bulldog" Bob Brown, King Kong Brody, "Bruiser" Bob Sweetan, and the Hollywood Blondes (Jerry Brown and Buddy Roberts). In St. Louis, I was billed as Chris Curtis from Green Bay, Wisconsin, and I worked as a babyface. In Kansas City, I also hailed from Green Bay and wrestled a lot of the same guys, but I was a heel.

Once I flew to St. Louis to tape a match against Bruiser Brody. His real name was Frank Goodish and he was extremely intelligent, but he was also extremely unpredictable. Still, when I wrestled Brody in St. Louis, he was very good to me. He was a big guy, about six foot five and close to three hundred pounds, but he moved like a gazelle. I learned very quickly that Brody was very appreciative of whatever the jobbers did to help him sell his moves. After our match, he came over and thanked me for putting him over. He may have been a little strange, but he was certainly a gentleman. At least to those who made him look good during a match. Woody Wilson, one of the jobbers on the rip, found out the hard way what happened if you crossed Brody in the ring. Wilson showed up ringside wearing a T-shirt several sizes too small. He was built like a beer barrel, with broomstick arms and legs, so on his frame the T-shirt looked ridiculous. To make matters worse, it said "Heavenly Perfection" in big letters on the front! It was a mistake to wear the T-shirt, but Wilson was never one to learn from his mistakes. One time, he told Verne Gagne he could bench press seventy-five pounds, and Verne almost killed him. Anyway, Brody stomps in, sees Wilson wearing that stupid T-shirt, and goes after him. Wilson never got a chance to take the thing off. Brody annihilated him in two minutes, and Wilson never knew what hit him.

Another funny thing happened around Wilson a few years later in Crown Point, Indiana. Wilson knew that a skinny little guy who worked outlaw shows as the Convict was putting on a house show of his own at Crown Point High School. Wilson dragged a bunch of us down there to be on the card. When we got there, it was a below-zero night in January, and the high school gym was packed. Well, we quickly found out that the Convict had advertised a main event with Sgt. Slaughter versus Moose Cholak, even though he never booked them! "Oh boy, this ought to be fun," I thought. "Wait until the crowd finds out they've been had!" When the lights went down for the main event, the Milwaukee jobber and power lifter Kenny Kasprzak walked out of the dressing room in jeans, work boots, and a flannel shirt cut off at the arms. The buzz in the gym got louder and angrier as Kasprzak was introduced as Little Moose, the nephew of the great Moose Cholak. Then I started laughing my butt off because people were expecting Sgt. Slaughter. Instead, Wilson came down the aisle with boots and a whip and wearing a Canadian Mountie hat. He was introduced as Sergeant Dallas Young, standing in for Slaughter. I thought there was gonna be a riot. The crowd was booing and throwing stuff in the ring. I have to give Wilson credit, though. He played the drill instructor bit to the hilt and even got on the microphone to make the fans madder! He kept blowing his whistle and snapping Little Moose on the butt with his whip. The fans started laughing and cheering and actually liked the match. I had once worked Wilson as the drill instructor at Federation Hall in Milwaukee, and I think he was born to play that character. He cracked me across the butt with a riding crop, and the crowd thought it was hysterical. Wilson really got over with the Indiana fans that night, and there's no doubt he saved the Convict from a world of trouble. If Wilson hadn't been so funny, the crowd would have demanded their money back.

There was always excitement and something new to look forward to at the Chase. For example, in May 1979, I was taping TV matches there when Pat O'Connor told the headliners not to use each other's finishing moves. Dory Funk Jr., a former NWA world champion, thought it would be funny to get O'Connor riled up a bit. Funk disobeyed O'Connor and used Harley Race's standing suplex and Bob Sweetan's pile driver while wrestling Ron McFarland. After each finish, Funk had McFarland kick out just in time. The dressing room upstairs had a one-way glass window that allowed us to see what was happening in the ring below. As you can imagine, O'Connor was going ballistic every time Funk did one of the other guys' moves. Sweetan, ever the comedian, said to O'Connor, "He just killed my finish." Then O'Connor had to watch as Funk finally made McFarland submit with a stupid, totally useless spinning toe hold. Funk came back to the dressing room and, with a perfectly straight face, asked O'Connor how the match looked. O'Connor just stared daggers at him.

After that show, Wilson, Fred Torres, and I hopped in a car to go work for Geigel in Kansas City. Nine hours into the trip, it was early Saturday morning, and we had to be at the TV studio by eight o'clock, so of course Wilson was speeding. A big Missouri state trooper who looked like a drill sergeant eventually pulled us over. The trooper ambled up to the driver's side and asked Wilson for his license and registration. Wilson had just gotten his license reinstated in Wisconsin on a provisional basis, so he shouldn't have been driving. After looking the documents over, the trooper starts talking, sounding like Jackie Gleason in *Smokey and the Bandit*. He says, "Uh, Woodrow, we're enforcing the fifty-five-mile-an-hour speed limit this weekend, and I got you going better than seventy! Can you explain that, Woodrow?" I laughed my butt off partly because the trooper kept calling him "Woodrow" and partly because Wilson was stuttering and stammering. Then the trooper asked, "Woodrow, what are you in such a hurry for?" When Wilson finally spoke, he said, "Well, sir, we're professional wrestlers and we're going to Kansas City to wrestle on TV, sir." This was the best part because the trooper took off his mirrored sunglasses and stared at Wilson. "Woodrow, you're a rascal, aren't you?" Wilson stammered again, "Yes, sir," which made me laugh even harder. "Well, what kind of wrestling do you do, Woodrow?" Wilson repeated that he and the rest of us were professional wrestlers going to Kansas City. The trooper started eyeing Wilson up and down and said, "You're kidding, right?" Torres and I are almost pissing our pants trying not to laugh. "Woodrow, do you mean to say you do that fake-ass rasslin?"

Wilson started to tell him it wasn't fake, and I'm thinking, "Okay, we have to be at the TV studio in an hour, and this dope wants to argue with the trooper on the legitimacy of professional wrestling." The trooper could have taken Wilson into custody on the spot because he didn't have enough money on him to cover the ticket. Torres and I weren't about to bail him out, either. I finally had enough and told the officer we'd been on the road nine hours and we were running late. I also told him that the outcome of a pro wrestling match is fixed, and for that reason, we had to be at the TV studio an hour before taping to go over our matches with the opponents. I apologized profusely for Wilson, and the trooper seemed to appreciate my honesty. He let Wilson off with a warning and told him to be more careful next time. Wilson peeled out of there, but did we go straight to the studio? No, instead Wilson insisted we stop at Kentucky Fried Chicken so he could order a bucket of chicken and a thirty-two-ounce drink!

Woody Wilson wasn't the greatest wrestler, but he knew how to sell a match.
LARRY WIDEN

Another trip I'll never forget is when Tom Stone, Cesar Pabón, Armando Rodriguez, and I all piled in my girlfriend Debbie's Buick and headed to Kansas City for some TV work. Debbie was my first love, and it was really sweet of her to let me use her car to drive three clowns to our job. I promised Debbie I would be extra careful with her car.

After we finished our shows, we got dressed and started for Milwaukee. I stopped for gas, and while I was filling the tank, Pabón, Stone, and Rodriguez ran into the store and bought a bunch of food and drinks for the trip. As I got up to sixty-five miles an hour, Stone pulled out a huge bottle of pomegranate juice and drank it so fast he made those hilarious chugging noises. He sounded like Curly from *The Three Stooges*. I was mad at Stone for sneaking all that crap in the car, so I watched him in the rearview mirror. Every time Stone took a swig of that damned juice, I slammed on the brakes. Pretty soon the front of his gray shirt was purple, and he was mad as hell. Stone got me back later, though, when I let Armando drive so I could sleep. Stone waited until I was snoring, then he slapped me across the chest as hard as he could. I screamed at the top of my lungs and almost clawed his eyes out!

It seemed like the longest car ride I'd ever taken, but finally I got home to Milwaukee. I gave Debbie a big hug and kiss and went to sleep. It must have been five minutes after I conked out when I heard her holler, "Christopher Joseph Multerer!" I thought, "Oh God, now what?" I found Debbie outside. She had her car doors open and fire in her eyes. When I looked in the back seat, I saw the problem. The guys had left all their McDonald's bags, beer cans, pomegranate juice bottles, forty-four-ounce sodas, candy wrappers, potato chip bags, and a bunch of other junk in the back seat. I cleaned out the car, got it washed and vacuumed, and bought a big bouquet of flowers for Debbie. She forgave me, but I was never allowed to take the car again.

Debbie was a nurse from Pike Lake, Minnesota, near Duluth,

and had family there. I met her while working security at Children's Hospital of Wisconsin in 1979. She invited me to meet her family on one of the weekends after I finished taping for TV in Minneapolis. One time, Debbie and her parents came to see a taping. I was wrestling Paul Ellering, whom the office wanted me to put over as the AWA's new babyface. During my match with Ellering, some woman in the audience kept yelling for him to break my arm. Debbie and her folks thought that was pretty funny, so they chimed in as well. Afterward, I met her family and they were very nice. Of course, her mom and dad had envisioned me as a knuckle-dragging cretin with a bad haircut and cauliflower ears. Much to their surprise and delight, Debbie introduced them to a devastatingly handsome man with a thick crop of dark, curly hair and a dazzling smile. I thought Debbie was "the one," but sadly, our relationship ended a few months later because she missed Duluth and wanted to move back to that area. It was a tough call for me not to go with her, but I had worked hard to get where I was, and I wanted to stay with wrestling.

In July 1979, I wrestled in a professional house show. Remember, in professional wrestling you want to land a TV job and then

A die-hard fan cheers during a 1979 match in Milwaukee. LARRY WIDEN

MAY 11, 1979, DAVENPORT TV

Pat Patterson and Ray Stevens beat Doug Somers and
  George Gadaski
Jesse Ventura beat Ted Wicker
Steve Olsonoski beat Fernando Torres
Paul Ellering beat Chris Curtis
Nick Bockwinkel beat Armando Rodriguez

MAY 19, 1979, DAVENPORT TV

Steve Olsonoski and Paul Ellering beat Doug Somers and
  Chris Curtis
Dick Reynolds beat Jesse Ventura (DQ)
Doug Gilbert beat Peter Lee
Nick Bockwinkel beat Tom Stone
Bobby Duncum beat George Gadaski

JUNE 2, 1979, DAVENPORT TV

Paul Ellering beat Fernando Torres
Jesse Ventura beat Armando Rodriguez
Greg Gagne beat Buck Zumhofe
Super Destroyer Mark II beat Cesar Pabón
Dick Reynolds beat Chris Curtis

get a house show, so this was a big deal for me. In front of a live crowd, I was matched against Dick Reynolds at the Minneapolis Auditorium.

I enjoyed house shows more than filming for TV mainly because wrestling for TV was all about finishing exactly on time. When I wrestled for TV, there always came a point in the match when I would be given a signal that meant I had sixty seconds to wrap it up. At first, Wally Karbo would stand outside the dressing room, and that meant "go to the finish." But some fans got wise to that, and the signal to finish changed. The timekeeper at ringside

JULY 15, 1979, MINNEAPOLIS AUDITORIUM—
MINNEAPOLIS, MINNESOTA

Greg Gagne beat AWA champion Nick Bockwinkel (DQ)
Ray Stevens beat Mad Dog Vachon (DQ)
Paul Ellering beat Jesse Ventura
Stan Hansen and Bobby Duncum beat Billy Robinson and
  Doug Gilbert
Super Destroyer Mark II beat Doug Gilbert
Dick Reynolds beat Chris Curtis

might tap his nose with a pencil, or the referee might tap me on the shoulder. Either way, it meant the same thing. In contrast, house shows gave new wrestlers like me a chance to learn the nuances of the business. For example, if I was doing a particular hold on an opponent and the crowd wasn't engaged, I'd switch to something else that would get them cheering or booing.

The energy from an audience is contagious. On a good night, there's also a measure of unpredictability. When I learned to pick up on the moods in the crowd, I became a better heel because I had more confidence in my ability to control the match. The babyface really doesn't have to do anything but walk out to the ring, smile and wave, maybe even sign a few autographs. The heel has the responsibility of inciting the crowd and raising the level of energy in the room. To do that, I would come out of the dressing room looking sullen or angry. If people tried to shake my hand or pat me on the back, I'd push them away. If someone said something derogatory, I'd find a way to belittle him in front of his friends. Once inside the ring, I'd cheat, break the rules, distract the referee, or pretend I had brass knuckles in my trunks. One of my best gimmicks was to plead for mercy when the babyface was finally getting his comeback on me. The crowd loved seeing me beg after all the crap

I pulled. Or, when I was getting too much heat, I'd scramble out of the ring and walk around until it was time to jump back in before the referee counted me out. People hated me for that! But that's what I was paid to do. My job was to make the babyface look good so he wouldn't have to cheat or fight dirty. All the feedback from the crowd made me try harder. I always wanted to walk out of the ring feeling like I had done my best work.

On August 21, 1979, my mom saw me wrestle for the first time. Earlier that day, I was goofing around with some people outside Larry Widen's apartment in Milwaukee when the brakes on a car locked up at the curb where we were standing. My mom yelled out the window, "The office called! They want you to wrestle tonight! I have your stuff!" The guys and I piled into the car, and my mom drove us to the back door of the Milwaukee Arena. It was only about ten blocks from Widen's apartment to the arena, but I think my mom drove us down there in less than sixty seconds. I asked her to stay and see the match, so she parked and picked up a complimentary ticket at the box office. She got a great seat, right at ringside! I dressed and was told I'd be wrestling Adrian Adonis, who was new to the Milwaukee territory. Of course, my job was to put him over. At one point during the match, Adonis threw me on the mat and started applying a series of spinning toe holds. It's a great move because it looks like the jobber's in a lot of pain. Suddenly, I hear a lady yelling from the front row, "Stop it! Stop it! Don't you know he's got bad knees?" I started laughing and Adrian said, "What the hell is that about?" I told him it was my mother. "Just make like you're working my knee and I'll sell it." We moved right in front of where my mom was sitting and Adrian just cranked on my knee. I was crying and begging, and both of us were trying not to laugh because every time we looked over at my mom, she was yelling at the referee to call the match. When I saw Adrian after that, we always had a good laugh about how we put it over on my mom.

JULY 7, 1979, DAVENPORT TV

Pat Patterson and Ray Stevens beat Butch Malone and
    Dick Reynolds
Billy Robinson beat Armando Rodriguez
Jesse Ventura beat Cesar Pabón
Greg Gagne beat AWA champion Nick Bockwinkel
Paul Ellering beat Chris Curtis

JULY 8, 1979, MINNEAPOLIS TV

Paul Ellering beat Ron McFarland
Super Destroyer Mark II beat Angel Rivera
Billy Robinson beat Chris Curtis
Greg Gagne beat Nick Bockwinkel

JULY 21, 1979, DAVENPORT TV

Paul Ellering beat Ron McFarland
Super Destroyer Mark II beat Angel Rivera
Billy Robinson beat Chris Curtis
Jesse Ventura beat Dick Reynolds

**SEPTEMBER 9, 1979, MINNEAPOLIS
AUDITORIUM—MINNEAPOLIS, MINNESOTA**

The Crusher and Greg Gagne beat Nick Bockwinkel and
    Bobby Duncum
Super Destroyer Mark II beat Billy Robinson (DQ)
Steve Olsonoski and Paul Ellering beat Jesse Ventura and
    Roger Kirby
Ron Ritchie beat Chris Curtis
Peter Sandor Szabo beat Kenny Jay

Wrestling Adrian
Adonis at the
Milwaukee Audi-
torium in 1979.
LARRY WIDEN

**SEPTEMBER 21, 1979, MILWAUKEE
AUDITORIUM—MILWAUKEE, WISCONSIN**

Super Destroyer Mark II and Mark III beat Billy Robinson
and Mad Dog Vachon
Bobo Brazil beat Bobby Duncum
Jesse Ventura beat Paul Ellering
Steve Olsonoski beat Peter Sandor Szabo
Adrian Adonis beat Chris Curtis

SEPTEMBER 22, 1979, DAVENPORT TV

Super Destroyer Mark II beat George Gadaski
Billy Robinson beat Kenny Jay
Nick Bockwinkel beat Harry Dragon
Greg Gagne beat Jerry Brown
Steve Olsonoski and Paul Ellering beat Puppy Dog Peloquin
and Chris Curtis

OCTOBER 21, 1979, MINNEAPOLIS TV

Adrian Adonis beat Kenny Jay
Steve Olsonoski beat Chris Curtis

Finding myself in a rush to get to a stadium or arena wasn't
all that out of the ordinary. For instance, in October 1979, Wally
Karbo asked me to wrestle in Chicago at the International Amphitheatre. "Sure," I said, "When?" "Tomorrow," Wally said, and
gave me the details. Now if you're wondering what's with all this
last-minute stuff, well, that's the way they do things in wrestling.
If you want to keep working, you don't say no. I learned that
lesson early, and I never said no when the office called. Whenever I had a chance to wrestle, I would cancel whatever I was
doing, grab my stuff, and go. I did it because wrestling was what
I wanted to do with my life, so I was willing to put up with how
the business worked.

When I got to Chicago, I found out why I had been booked
at the last minute. I was paired with fifty-five-year-old Rev. Tim
Hampton, a black wrestler from Benton Harbor, Michigan.
Hampton got into the business decades earlier with some help
from Bobo Brazil. Because Hampton had taken to managing the

In the men's room getting ready for my first wrestling match at Chicago's
famed International Amphitheatre. I felt like I had arrived. LARRY WIDEN

Rev. Tim Hampton
looks on as the ref
checks to be certain
I didn't bring a for-
eign object into the
ring. LARRY WIDEN

Valiant Brothers and Ernie Ladd, he had become a bit of a stiff in
the ring. That's where I came in. It was up to me to carry Hampton
in our tag team match against Wilbur Snyder and Spike Huber,
who was Dick the Bruiser's son-in-law.

By now it should be obvious how things worked in professional wrestling. You could either be related to someone and get
work, or you could invest some money somewhere and make that
angle pay off. Verne Gagne, for example, had invested money in
an operation run by Snyder and Bruiser. They needed a job man
not only for Hampton but for Snyder as well, who was the same
age as Hampton. I had my work cut out for me. Lucky for me,
Huber was a good worker. He and I took all the bumps and high
spots, making it easier on the older guys.

After my match in Chicago, I went to Ronnie's Steak Palace
with some friends who had come down from Milwaukee to watch
me wrestle. Dinner wasn't the best part of the night, though. No,
the best thing about the Chicago job was that it confirmed what
I already knew. I'd been given the chance to be successful in the
business of professional wrestling, and the people I worked for

thought I was doing a good job. I was getting a lot of work, which made me more confident that wrestling is what I wanted to do for a living.

After that night, I started getting regular work from the AWA. One afternoon, Karbo said they needed somebody for a battle royal at the St. Paul Civic Center. "When?" I asked. "Tonight," was the answer. I grabbed my gear and was on a plane within an hour. A driver picked me up in St. Paul, and we headed to the Civic Center. When I made it to the dressing room, I learned that Gagne and Karbo had just hired a new guy in the territory, Dino Bravo, and they needed a jobber to put him over in a big way. Karbo said, "All we want is a really good sixty-second match."

As I walked out to the ring to face Bravo, two goofballs in the bleachers started giving me a hard time. "Curtis, you pussy. You stink," they said. I walked over and replied, "Hey guys, I'll be back in exactly one minute and then I'm gonna beat the living shit outta both of you!" I got in the ring, and as soon as the match started, Bravo turned his back on me. I hit him from behind and he reversed me into the turnbuckle, flipped me twice, then

At the airport in Milwaukee, getting on a four-seater bound for Minneapolis. During the flight, a snowstorm forced the pilot to make an emergency landing.
LARRY WIDEN

finished up with two big body slams. Of course, I worked it like Bravo was killing me and the crowd ate it up. Finally, Bravo put me in an airplane spin, dropped me, and pinned me, all in sixty seconds! I acted like I was dizzy from the spin and held my back like it hurt. When Bravo put his arms up in the air, the audience went crazy. As soon as I got out of the ring, I walked toward the bleachers and the two guys that had heckled me. They jumped up and ran away! That's the heel's job, to get the crowd involved so the match goes over big.

To be honest, I was nervous about wrestling Dino Bravo because he had a bit of a reputation as a shooter with the job men. Bravo had purposefully stepped on the face of Jim Evans during a match with the intention of breaking Evans's nose. A couple other jobbers suffered similar treatment, and Bret "the Hitman" Hart claimed Bravo cracked his ribs. There was never any reason for a star wrestler to intentionally harm a job man because job men were there to make the stars look good. There was talk that Bravo's behavior stemmed from steroid use that had escalated to dangerous levels as he sought to become the strongest man in

---

OCTOBER 23, 1979, ST. PAUL AUDITORIUM— ST. PAUL, MINNESOTA

André the Giant won a battle royal that included card
    wrestlers and Peter Sandor Szabo, Moose Morowski,
    Greg Gagne, Billy Robinson, Mad Dog Vachon,
    Lord Alfred Hayes, and Super Destroyer Mark II
André the Giant beat Super Destroyer Mark II
Jesse Ventura beat Steve Olsonoski
Adrian Adonis beat Paul Ellering
Dino Bravo beat Chris Curtis
Ron Ritchie beat George Gadaski

the world. In 1986, Bravo chased stardom when he joined Vince McMahon Jr.'s WWF. Bravo became part of "Luscious" Johnny Valiant's stable of wrestlers that included Brutus the Beefcake and Greg "the Hammer" Valentine. He routinely performed feats of strength, such as doing pushups with 450-pound weights on his back or staging bench pressing contests before his matches. At the 1988 Royal Rumble, Bravo nearly broke the world's record by benching close to seven hundred pounds.

Bravo left the WWF in 1991 after a fight with McMahon. When he did, he found that he couldn't sustain a high standard of living. Within a few months, Bravo was reportedly earning a lot of money selling stolen cigarettes in Canada. On March 10, 1993, the forty-four-year-old Bravo was shot to death in his home. He was shot seven times in the head and ten times in the body. The assassin was never apprehended.

Unfortunately, professional wrestling at the time attracted some people who, like Bravo, were out to harm others in the ring. I wrestled more than a few of them. It's one thing to be lazy or a stiff in the ring who's hard to put over. Some guys laid in punches and chops or put a little extra on their kicks. I could handle that. Exhibiting total disregard for a job man, though, by trying to hurt him while he's in a defensive position, was something else altogether.

Khosrow Vaziri was the kind of wrestler who would hurt an opponent for no apparent reason. Vaziri wrestled as the Iron Sheik, turning professional in 1972 with the help of Gagne and Billy Robinson. Vaziri was a member of the 1968 Iranian Olympic wrestling team before moving to the United States shortly afterward. In 1971, he won the Amateur Athletic Union Greco-Roman championship. Over the first ten years of his professional career, Vaziri earned a reputation, primarily by using a signature finisher called the camel clutch. To apply the camel clutch, Vaziri forced his opponent face down on the mat and squatted on his upper back. Vaziri then grabbed the helpless jobber by the chin and pulled back as hard as he could until the opponent tapped out. Yet even after his opponent had submitted, Vaziri often pushed his opponent's face into the mat upon releasing him, causing needless injuries such as broken noses and knocked out teeth.

Manny "the Raging Bull" Fernandez, like Khosrow Vaziri, had little regard for job men and their safety. Fernandez played football at West Texas State and had a short stint in the NFL in the 1970s. He wore an outrageous mullet haircut that included a white spot on the back, so it looked like a skunk was on his head. Fernandez trained under Terry Funk and Dick Murdoch, two of the best workers in the business, but they apparently forgot to teach Fernandez that wrestlers are not in the ring to do real harm to their opponents. The Raging Bull showed no mercy to jobbers. When he was in the ring with them, he inflicted pain whenever he could. He seemed to enjoy surprising his opponent with big, unexpected, and painful moves.

Frank DeFalco found this out the hard way when he was matched against Fernandez during an AWA television taping in Milwaukee in 1989. I was talking with DeFalco when Fernandez walked by. DeFalco asked him what the finish would be. Fernandez looked DeFalco up and down, and said, "You'll know it when you see it." I felt really bad for DeFalco, because an answer like that is a sign of bad things to come.

DeFalco knew he was in for trouble when he climbed into the ring with Fernandez. Fernandez's finisher was a flying forearm to the face, the same move used by Tito Santana. Unlike Santana, however, Fernandez didn't pull the punch before hurting his opponent. Fernandez landed the move on DeFalco, who came back to the dressing room cross-eyed. DeFalco never wrestled again, which was probably a good thing.

More than Viziri and Fernandez, the Road Warriors, a two-man destruction crew composed of Joe Laurinaitis, who went by

"Animal," and Michael Hegstrand, who went by "Hawk," went out of their way to make life miserable for job men. In fact, when the Road Warriors were at their peak in 1982 and 1983, any jobber with half a brain wouldn't show up for a TV taping if he was scheduled to wrestle them. Laurinaitis and Hegstrand were working as bouncers at Gramma B's, a bar in Minneapolis, when they were discovered by former pro wrestler Eddie Sharkey. Sharkey was an industry legend who once waved a pistol at Verne Gagne for hitting on his wife, who wrestled as Princess Little Cloud. Sharkey taught Laurinaitis and Hegstrand the tricks of the trade, and they quickly found lucrative work with Georgia Championship Wrestling.

The Road Warriors dressed like characters from the *Mad Max* movies, wearing menacing face paint and their hair in mohawks. The fans in Georgia went crazy for them. Weighing a combined 545 pounds and managed by Paul Ellering, the Road Warriors were a force to be reckoned with. Ellering, whom I had wrestled the night Debbie and her parents watched me in Minneapolis, came to the AWA in 1979 as a babyface. He was a former junior powerlifting champion who could deadlift more than seven hundred pounds. Ellering was as smart as he was strong, with an IQ of 162. Yet knee injuries set his wrestling career back. Eventually, Ellering made his way to Memphis and became a heel, bleaching his hair blond and taking on an unfriendly persona.

It was at this point that Atlanta promoter Ole Anderson hired Ellering to run the Road Warriors. Anderson had come up with the idea for the Road Warriors, which he envisioned as a cross between characters from *Mad Max* and Hells Angels motorcycle outlaws. With no empathy whatsoever, Anderson had spent his career beating up job men, so it made sense that he would teach the Road Warriors to do the same. Because the Road Warriors were too green and too stupid to do anything but what Anderson told them to do, Laurinaitis and Hegstrand became so feared that fans and other wrestlers were literally terrified of them. That they couldn't wrestle was immaterial—what mattered was the pain awaiting those who stepped into the ring with them. The Road Warriors bench pressed unsuspecting jobbers over their heads and threw them over the top rope to land on a concrete floor. I watched them drop Curt Hennig face first on the mat before Hennig had a chance to prepare himself for the fall. In Milwaukee, I saw Hegstrand body slam Dick the Bruiser, who was fifty-five years old at the time, into the mat with enough force to seriously injure the legendary wrestler. Dick the Bruiser, along with the Crusher, was really angry with the way the Road Warriors behaved in the ring, and in a way, Laurinaitis and Hegstrand were lucky. When the Crusher and Dick the Bruiser were at their best, they would have settled things with Animal and Hawk right in front of the fans.

Eventually, the Road Warriors wore out their welcome. Paul Ellering retired from professional wrestling to run a lakeside restaurant in Minnesota. Laurinaitis became a born-again Christian and devoted himself to his family. His son, James, had a successful career in the NFL as a linebacker. Michael Hegstrand died of a heart attack in 2003.

After I wrestled Dino Bravo in October, I competed in my first big battle royal, held in November 1979 at the Brown County Veterans Memorial Arena in Green Bay. When it came to the battle royals, the AWA would usually designate somebody onsite—one of the veterans such as Nick Bockwinkel or Greg Gagne—to determine the order of how the guys were going to get bounced out of the ring. There were fourteen wrestlers that night, including Jesse Ventura, André the Giant, the Crusher, Mad Dog Vachon, Billy Robinson, and Greg Gagne. And then there was me! If you think I wasn't amazed and proud as hell to be there with all those stars, guess again. And I wasn't the first one thrown out! Steve Olsonoski went out first, followed by Buck Zumhofe. I was the third guy tossed out of the ring. That I was third to go made me so proud, because my being there meant that the people I worked for thought I was good at what I did.

Anyway, as the battle royal started, I followed Bobby Heenan, Mad Dog Vachon, and the other heels toward one side of the ring. After we fired up the crowd, the babyfaces came out and arranged themselves on the opposite side of the ring. Well, there I was, twenty-two years old, standing in a professional wrestling ring with guys I'd been watching on television and admiring since I was a kid. Then I heard the bell ring. The first thing I saw was Mad Dog Vachon, looking like he wanted to kill me. As he came up, he whispered, "Stop me. Rake my eyes." I did as I was told and threw Mad Dog into a corner, where I started working him over. Mad Dog sold my performance like a pro, because Mad Dog could have beat up anybody except André the Giant. As Mad Dog was rubbing his eyes, acting like I had blinded him, Billy Robinson, the guy who had tried to stretch me in one of my first matches, grabbed my shoulder. I thought I was gonna get pasted, but Robinson just gave me a tiny smile and moved away. In that moment I felt like, "Yeah, I passed the test, I'm in with these guys." It finally dawned on me that I could hack it as a pro wrestler. It was just like Bockwinkel and Stevens had told me when I first wrestled Robinson: "Nothing personal, just part of getting into the fraternity." By the time Olsonoski and Zumhofe had been tossed out of the ring, the Crusher had found me. He said, "When are you supposed to go?" "Now," I replied. Without missing a beat, the Crusher grabbed my hair and ran me over the top rope, sending me falling to the ring apron and onto the arena floor. My first battle royal with superstars ended there, and the whole experience was nothing short of a blast.

NOVEMBER 11, 1979, BROWN COUNTY VETERANS MEMORIAL ARENA— GREEN BAY, WISCONSIN

The Crusher won a fourteen-man battle royal for $20,000 by eliminating Adrian Adonis, Buck Zumhofe, Steve Olsonoski, Chris Curtis, Billy Robinson, Paul Ellering, Greg Gagne, Super Destroyer Mark III, Buddy Wolff, Mad Dog Vachon, André the Giant, Jesse Ventura, and Dino Bravo

André the Giant beat Jesse Ventura

Mad Dog Vachon beat Super Destroyer Mark II

Dino Bravo beat Buddy Wolff

Greg Gagne drew Steve Olsonoski

Adrian Adonis beat Paul Ellering

NOVEMBER 17, 1979, DAVENPORT TV

Dino Bravo beat Chris Curtis

Hollywood Nelson beat Armando Rodriguez

Buck Zumhofe beat Nacho Berrera

Nick Bockwinkel beat Harry Dragon

DECEMBER 9, 1979, DAVENPORT TV

Dino Bravo beat Herman Schaefer

Adrian Adonis and Jesse Ventura beat Buck Zumhofe and Fernando Torres

Greg Gagne beat Chris Curtis

Buddy Wolff beat Ron Ritchie

Super Destroyer Mark II beat Peter Sandor Szabo

DECEMBER 16, 1979, DAVENPORT TV

Steve Olsonoski and Paul Ellering beat Chris Curtis and
   Puppy Dog Peloquin
Greg Gagne beat Jimmy Brown
Jesse Ventura beat Peter Sandor Szabo
Billy Robinson beat Kenny Jay
Nick Bockwinkel beat Sonny Driver

DECEMBER 16, 1979, MINNEAPOLIS TV

Dino Bravo beat Chris Curtis
Adrian Adonis beat Ricky Hunter
The Crusher beat Jimmy Brown
Super Destroyer Mark II beat Ron Ritchie

DECEMBER 23, 1979, MINNEAPOLIS TV

Adrian Adonis beat Kenny Jay
Steve Olsonoski beat Chris Curtis
Greg Gagne beat Jimmy Brown
Ron Ritchie beat Sonny Driver
Buddy Wolff beat Al Ringo

Chapter 5

Around the time I was wrestling in the battle royal in Green Bay, Steve Hall moved to Louisiana to run job men for Cowboy Bill Watts, a former professional football player and professional wrestler. Watts first wrestled for Verne Gagne, then later for Vince McMahon Sr. In 1979, Watts bought the Tri-State Wrestling circuit from Oklahoma-based promoter Leroy McGuirk and renamed it Mid-South Wrestling. Mid-South's territory included Arkansas as well as Louisiana and Mississippi. Watts was considered one of the best promoters in the country, and his shows drew well. He alternated small-town house shows with an occasional event at a huge arena, including a 1980 main event at the Louisiana Superdome featuring a "blinded" Junkyard Dog against one of the Fabulous Freebirds, Michael Hayes, which drew nearly thirty thousand fans. In 1982, Watts expanded and bought the Oklahoma territory from McGuirk. He also cut a deal with Texas promoter Paul Boesch to bring some Mid-South stars to the Sam Houston Coliseum in Houston.

After a short-lived football career with the Houston Oilers and the Minnesota Vikings, six foot three, 280-pound Bill Watts became a pro wrestler with the help of former University of Oklahoma teammate Wahoo McDaniel. Under the name Cowboy Bill Watts, he moved to New York City's WWWF in 1962 and became the tag team partner of heavyweight champ Bruno Sammartino. Watts asked several times for a chance to

wrestle Sammartino for the title, but WWWF promoters refused. During a match, Watts turned on Sammartino, and the
two became bitter enemies. Sammartino retained the title in a
sell-out match at Madison Square Garden, and Watts left the
territory for San Francisco. He feuded with Ray "the Crippler"
Stevens in several memorable matches and then embarked on
a successful tour of Japan.

When Watts returned to America in 1967, he accepted
Verne Gagne's offer to join the AWA. Watts was a huge draw
in Chicago, St. Louis, Indianapolis, Milwaukee, Davenport,
and Omaha. His popularity was boosted by feuds with Gagne
and NWA champion Gene Kiniski. Matches with Waldo Von
Eric, Boris Malenko, Dusty Rhodes, Ox Baker, and other regional stars followed.

In the mid-1970s, Watts began booking matches for Florida
promoter Eddie Graham. Within several years, he formed his
own circuit, Mid-South Wrestling. He ran shows in Texas,
Mississippi, Louisiana, and Oklahoma with "Hacksaw" Jim
Duggan, Steve "Dr. Death" Williams, and Sylvester "Junkyard
Dog" Ritter. Watts ran the Mid-South territory the way Verne
Gagne ran the AWA. He employed ex-football players and
college wrestlers and trained his guys in the art of professional
wrestling. Amateur wrestlers aren't always successful in transitioning to the professional ranks, and Watts had little patience
for poor performance in the ring. Job men in the Mid-South
had to learn how to work in a hurry, and veteran heels such as
Ox Baker, Apache Bull Ramos, Ernie Ladd, and Mike George
were great teachers.

Watts sold Mid-South Wrestling in 1987 and went to work
for World Championship Wrestling (WCW). He was forced
out in 1993 when baseball legend Hank Aaron, an executive
with WCW's parent company, got wind of racial slurs Watts
had made during an interview.

Once Steve Hall got settled, he was going to give me regular work there. That gave me about a month to finish up my remaining commitments with the AWA in Minneapolis. It also gave me enough time to wrestle in a match that put me in hot water with Verne and Greg Gagne. One night, I arrived at the Milwaukee Auditorium and found that I was supposed to wrestle a new guy, Peter Sandor Szabo. When I walked over to introduce myself to him, I quickly discovered that he didn't speak or understand English! Communication is obviously key in professional wrestling, so I didn't know what to do. How was I supposed to tell Peter what the high spots and the finish would be? I didn't have much time to think about it. Szabo and I went to the ring, and I just hoped he would be savvy enough to respond to some nonverbal signals and everything would be okay.

That was too much to ask of Szabo. We had no business performing in front of people being as unprepared as we were. Right away we locked up and got our signals crossed. I came off the ropes expecting Szabo to throw me, but he turned away. I didn't know what to do, so in a split second, I made the decision to change directions and fell into the turnbuckle. That was about the lamest move ever. The audience started booing and yelling and, as luck would have it, Greg Gagne was standing outside the dressing room, watching the match. When I came to the dressing room after the match, Gagne was waiting for me. He was livid. He started yelling at me, "What the hell were you doing out there, Curtis? Are you trying to kill this business?" I tried to explain that Szabo didn't understand English, but Gagne was so mad he wouldn't listen.

I left the auditorium that night knowing I was in trouble because Greg Gagne told his dad everything. I was also mad because Gagne refused to assume any responsibility for giving me an untried opponent. The next day, I flew to Minneapolis to do TV. When I walked into the dressing room, I saw Verne and Greg

Gagne in the corner. They saw me and motioned for me to come over. Verne said he had heard about last night and wanted to know what happened. I thought, "Oh, man, my wrestling career may be over right now." Verne was very protective of his business. His number one rule was that you didn't expose anything to the crowd. By the look in his eye, I figured Verne was going to have me stretched or fired, or both. I glanced at Greg, but he wasn't saying anything. He didn't have to. His old man said it all: "Are you trying to kill this business, Curtis?" I said, "Of course not! Why would I want to do that?" I gave Verne a repeat version of what I had said to Greg the night before. "Szabo doesn't speak English and I was trying to call the match in the dressing room and he didn't understand me, so we had to wing it," I said. "I'm really sorry about the bad show, Verne. I tried to do the right thing." Verne looked at me for what seemed about a minute. Then he turned and walked away.

I taped my matches and showered in the dressing room, all the while figuring it might be the last time I'd ever do it. Afterward, I found Wally Karbo in his office and told him I was leaving the territory to work for Cowboy Bill Watts. Wally simply said, "Okay, then." Nobody said anything to me as I left. You know how you get that sick feeling in the pit of your stomach when something bad happens? Well, I had that and more. The AWA shit list was no place for a professional wrestler. Still, I kept thinking that in two weeks I was going to Louisiana to work with Steve Hall. I hoped the black cloud I felt hanging over my head would stay behind in Milwaukee. The Szabo thing wasn't my fault, but part of being a jobber is to roll with the punches inside the ring as well as outside of it.

That said, in all my dealings with Greg Gagne, he was a good guy to work for. All told, I probably wrestled him more than anyone else during my time in the AWA. I also wrestled him once during the short time he teamed up with Jerry Blackwell. Gagne

With referee Marty Miller and ring announcer Gene Okerlund, waiting to
wrestle Buck Zumhofe at the TV studio in Minneapolis. LARRY WIDEN

was one of the greatest babyfaces in the business. He was a good
worker, light in the ring, and could sell the moves. Gagne made
me a better heel, and I learned a lot from him. He wasn't the
biggest guy—his weight stayed around 210—but he could body
slam a three-hundred-pound opponent. He also had a bit of a
temper and would let me know when I screwed up, but he was
a gentleman outside the ring, taking after his dad in that regard.

By the end of 1979, I had completed my plans to move south.
I leased a small, furnished apartment in Baton Rouge, Louisiana,
as a base from which to work. When I told my parents I was going
to work in Louisiana, my dad said, "Great." My mom just rolled
her eyes and said, "Twelve years of Catholic schooling so you can
become a wrestler?"

On December 26, a Wednesday, I was getting ready to head
out when Hall called me with the weekly booking sheet. It was a
good thing, too, because I was planning to drive straight through
to Baton Rouge from Milwaukee. Instead, I drove all night to

DECEMBER 14, 1979, MILWAUKEE
AUDITORIUM—MILWAUKEE, WISCONSIN

AWA champion Nick Bockwinkel beat Greg Gagne
Adrian Adonis and Jesse Ventura beat the Crusher and
   Steve Olsonoski
Dino Bravo beat Super Destroyer Mark II
Mad Dog Vachon vs. Super Destroyer Mark II (no contest
   [NC])
Buck Zumhofe drew Ron Ritchie
Peter Sandor Szabo beat Chris Curtis

Memphis, taking Highway 61 from there to Greenville, Mississippi. I pulled up in front of a National Guard armory late in the
afternoon. That Thursday night, I wrestled Hall, and on Friday, I
moved to Greenwood, Mississippi, where I wrestled Ricky Fields.
It was another four days before I was able to offload my belong-
ings at the apartment in Baton Rouge.

As I sat in my car in front of the armory, I wondered what
I had gotten myself into. Back home, working for the AWA, I
was wrestling in Green Bay, Milwaukee, Chicago, and Minneapolis, not cow towns in Mississippi. On top of that, the AWA
was flying me to the Twin Cities to tape my matches. They gave
me eighty-five dollars for each television match and $150 for ten
minutes in the ring at a house show. Working for Watts was a bit
of a comedown. On average, I'd make twenty-five to fifty dollars
a night. Watts didn't pay jobbers for doing TV matches either. I
probably should have asked Hall a few more questions before
taking the job.

Cowboy Bill Watts's circuit consisted of smaller towns in
Louisiana and Mississippi. Through them, Watts ran weekly or
biweekly shows depending on what the market would bear. I

watched Watts on television as a kid when he wrestled for Verne Gagne in the late 1960s. I liked him, only because I was too young or too stupid to know any better.

Watts was a tough bastard with an ego the size of his native Oklahoma. I found that out quickly when I picked him up from the Baton Rouge airport and drove him to a house show in Lake Charles, Louisiana. "Colonel" Buck Robley, who did the bookings for Watts, had asked me if I wanted to make extra money by chauffeuring Watts around. What I got was two hours of chin music from Watts yakking on and on about himself and his exploits. He complained that Verne Gagne never gave him the AWA world championship and bragged that he and Bruno Sammartino had broken box office records in New York City. Worst of all, Watts screwed me on the payday! When I dropped Watts off in Lake Charles, he threw five dollars at me and said, "Hey man, thanks a lot."

Watts ran his territory like Verne Gagne ran his. Watts had a roster that was stacked with tough guys and shooters. His guys were expected to lift weights at Foxy's Health Club in Baton Rouge, and Watts gave them hell if they didn't at least pretend to work out there. The only one who didn't have to lift was Robley, who had the worst physique I ever saw on a wrestler. Robley was skinny legged and pigeon-toed, with a pot belly and no muscles in his arms! His long hair and beard made him look like an old Confederate soldier, and a deep, gravelly voice with a Foghorn Leghorn southern drawl rounded out the desired effect. Robley was a great worker in the ring, though, and could really sell a match. Even better, he was a nice guy who looked after the jobbers.

Robley and Watts couldn't stand each other. Watts kept him around because Robley had a great mind for the business and knew how to cook up some intriguing storylines. For example, the crowds in the smaller Mississippi towns were mostly African American. One night, the main event was a tag team match featuring Robley and a popular black babyface wrestler named King

Cobra, taking on the Fabulous Freebirds tag team of Terry Gordy and Michael Hayes. The Freebirds wore sequined jackets with Confederate flags on them to get the crowd worked up. The finish they came up with was to throw Robley out of the ring and run his head into the ringpost. As Robley laid on the floor pretending to be unconscious, the Freebirds double-teamed King Cobra and beat on him until the Junkyard Dog ran into the ring and saved the day. The audience was going out of their minds the whole time. Things got so out of hand that Gordy and Hayes literally ran from the ring and out of the building, where they jumped into a car and sped off. It took a lot of guts to pull that whole thing off because those southerners really bought the storylines. If the Junkyard Dog hadn't appeared to bail out King Cobra, the Freebirds never would have made it out of the place in one piece!

Next it was off to Shreveport, Louisiana, where I taped TV matches at the studio. Then it was onto to Alexandria, Louisiana, where I wrestled Mark Totten. Totten was fun to hang out with because he had gone to high school in Bay Village, Ohio, with a cousin of mine. Totten was a state heavyweight wrestling champion and played a brief stint with the New England Patriots before getting into pro wrestling.

Working nightly house shows got me acquainted with Mid-South Wrestling and its territories in a hurry. After every house show, I came away feeling like I had learned something new. Because I still wasn't experienced enough to be a heel, Mid-South had me working as a babyface. I was still Chris Curtis (although I was billed as being from Green Bay), but I was there to put the headliner heels across. I wrestled five nights a week on the circuit, then taped television matches in Shreveport on Saturday mornings.

My average week went something like this. Typically, on Monday night I'd be in New Orleans for a house show. Then Tuesday was an off day. Next, the Wednesday house show would be in either Jackson or Vicksburg, Mississippi. From there, I would

I wrestled the Junk-
yard Dog a number
of times during my
career in Cowboy
Bill Watts's territory.
CENTRAL STATES
WRESTLING

wrestle in Greenville, Mississippi, or Lafayette, Louisiana, on Thursday. Friday nights were for house shows in Shreveport so we could be in town to tape TV matches on Saturdays. Every Saturday evening, we'd stay in Louisiana, doing shows in Alexandria, Slidell, or Loranger before having the day off Sunday. Come Monday, the whole thing would start over. It sounds hectic, but working the house shows night after night provided me a valuable education. In short order, I learned how to open matches, do bigger bumps, and be a better finisher.

In my best week, I made about $300, and in my worst week I made around $125. Four or five of us traveled together and shared gas and lodging to keep expenses low. House shows in the smaller towns would usually pay twenty-five or thirty dollars a night, and in the bigger towns I might make fifty dollars. Headliners such as the Fabulous Freebirds or the Junkyard Dog got a guaranteed salary for their appearances. My compensation was based on attendance. Other than the main eventers, the only guys making any real money at Mid-South were Bill Watts and Buck Robley.

The guys I wrestled most often during my time with Mid-South were Ox Baker, Apache Bull Ramos, Ernie Ladd, Ben Alexander, Michael Blood, the Junkyard Dog, Mike George, Tank Patton, and a few others. Ox Baker—his real name was Doug—stood six foot five and weighed 310 pounds. A bald head, wild eyebrows, and huge Fu Manchu mustache made Baker look positively demonic. Prior to coming to Mid-South, Baker had worked for the AWA in Minneapolis, Dick the Bruiser in Chicago, the Sheik in Detroit and Toronto, and Johnny Powers in Cleveland and Toledo. Baker's big finish was the heart punch, delivered with a taped fist. He even had a part in the movie *Escape from New York*, doing battle against Kurt Russell. I wrestled Baker many times in the Mid-South and loved it because he was light as a feather in the ring. One night in Alexandria, my shoulder was bothering me. During the match, Baker started to put me in an arm lock, and I said, "Ox, put me in a headlock, my shoulder is killing me." He clicked his dentures in and out and winked. I started to laugh, then I noticed Watts watching the match from the back of the house. Watts hated Baker. I thought, "Ah, shit, one or both of us is gonna get fired." But Watts didn't say anything when Baker and I got to the dressing room. It had been a great match, and Watts knew it.

Baker was good for a laugh. One Friday night, five of us stayed in a Shreveport hotel room so we could tape TV matches there the next morning. Two guys took one of the queen beds, and Ben Alexander and I took the floor. Then Baker came in with his girlfriend and got in the other queen bed. Let me tell you, it was a toss-up between Baker and his date when it came to who was better looking. It was quiet for a little while, then Baker started kissing her. Alexander followed suit, making smooching noises while the rest of us burst out laughing. The girl got upset and left,

Baker on her heels. They didn't come back, and nobody slept in that bed.

Sometimes the funniest things happened in the car while driving to or from the matches. On the way to Baton Rouge late one night, I was really tired so I let Alexander drive while I slept. Alexander, from North Carolina, told stories with an exaggerated southern drawl that made me laugh so hard I'd cry. That night, I think he was mad at me for falling asleep while he was talking. As I slept, I was jolted awake by a huge slap across my chest and the sound of Alexander yelling, "Mad dog, mad dog!" I jumped

Ox Baker was one of the best workers in the business. It looked like he was killing me during our matches, but I never felt a thing. MID-SOUTH WRESTLING

so hard I hit the windshield. Alexander was laughing so hard he went off the road and almost hit a tree. I never let him drive my car again.

The Junkyard Dog was a barrel of laughs on the road as well. He'd eat all kinds of fast food, then throw his trash out the car window. Once, in Mississippi, he tossed a huge bag of McDonald's garbage on the highway while driving seventy miles an hour. The bag flew behind us and landed right in front of a state trooper's cruiser. That little stunt set the Junkyard Dog back $200 in fines, and even better, the trooper made him get out of the car and pick up his trash.

I didn't have a lot of real friends in Louisiana, so I kept in touch with some of the guys I knew from the Midwest. One of my favorites in the AWA was Lord Alfred Hayes. Hayes was a talented British amateur wrestler with an extensive background in judo. When he turned pro, Hayes quickly established himself as one of the greatest heels in the business. In addition, Hayes was a great talker, and his interviews on the weekly television shows were fabulous. Once, when we were in town together, I brought up an angle that he and Verne Gagne had concocted in 1975. Hayes was going to start a feud with fellow British wrestler Billy Robinson, who was a popular babyface. During a Minneapolis television taping, Robinson was presented with a picture of himself from little Betty Button, a patient at a children's hospital. Robinson's hair was permed in ringlets at that time, and he had a slightly crossed eye from an injury suffered when he was a kid. Here's the funny part. There was no Betty Button. The picture was drawn by Alfred himself! It was the funniest damn thing I've ever seen. Hayes drew Robinson with wild, curly black hair and two crossed eyes. Producer Al DeRusha and a woman from the AWA officially presented the picture to Robinson while the cameras rolled. Hayes then jumped into the ring, made fun of the picture, and ripped it to shreds before clobbering Robinson over the head with a wooden easel. It was classic pro wrestling theater, and fans all over the territory went wild, believing that a sick child had drawn the picture. Hayes got so much heat for that stunt that he was able to play it out for a year. A few years later, Verne Gagne had Hayes wrestle as a babyface, creating a huge feud between Hayes and Bobby Heenan. The matches between them were great, in part because Heenan did a great job selling Hayes. Heenan usually ended up outside the ring, and when Hayes and the referee poked their heads through the ropes, Heenan smashed a folding chair over their heads! Hayes and I remained friends when I left the AWA to work the Mid-South. He was a true gentleman. We kept in touch on a regular basis until 2005, when Hayes died from a stroke while living in Texas.

While working in Lafayette, Louisiana, I drew the short straw and had to wrestle Mike Bowyer. I was uneasy about this because

JANUARY 3, 1980, LAFAYETTE, LOUISIANA

Junkyard Dog vs. Ernie Ladd
Mike Sharpe vs. Bob Sweetan
Jake Roberts vs. Sonny Driver
Steve Hall beat Chris Curtis

JANUARY 5, 1980, ALEXANDRIA, LOUISIANA

Bill Watts beat Mike George to win Mid-South North
    American title
Bob Sweetan vs. Mike Sharpe (NC)
Terry Gordy and Michael Hayes beat Buck Robley and
    King Cobra
Junkyard Dog beat Gino Hernandez
Ted DiBiase beat Mike Bowyer
Ox Baker beat Chris Curtis
Bull Ramos beat Mark Totten

JANUARY 9, 1980, JACKSON, MISSISSIPPI

Terry Gordy and Michael Hayes vs. Buck Robley and
 Junkyard Dog (NC)
Ted DiBiase beat Mike George
Bob Sweetan beat Ricky Fields
Bull Ramos beat Charlie Cook
Mike Sharpe beat Ben Alexander
Ox Baker beat Chris Curtis

JANUARY 10, 1980, LAFAYETTE, LOUISIANA

Terry Gordy and Michael Hayes beat Bill Watts and
 Buck Robley
Bob Sweetan beat Charlie Cook
Ted DiBiase beat Ox Baker
Bull Ramos beat Chris Curtis
Mark Totten beat Ben Alexander

JANUARY 12, 1980, SLIDELL, LOUISIANA

Bill Watts beat Bob Sweetan
Steve Hall beat Chris Curtis
Mike Blood drew Ben Alexander
King Cobra and Ricky Fields beat Tank Patton and
 Mike Bowyer

JANUARY 18, 1980, SHREVEPORT, LOUISIANA

Ernie Ladd beat Mike Sharpe to win Mid-South
 Louisiana title
Buck Robley and Junkyard Dog beat Terry Gordy and
 Michael Hayes
Ted DiBiase beat Ox Baker
Bull Ramos beat Chris Curtis
Mike Blood beat Sonny Driver
Mike Bowyer beat Steve Hall

JANUARY 19, 1980, ALEXANDRIA, LOUISIANA

Mike George beat Bill Watts to win Mid-South North
American title

Mike Sharpe beat Bob Sweetan

Ted DiBiase beat Ox Baker

Buck Robley and Junkyard Dog beat Terry Gordy and
Michael Hayes

Cowboy Lang beat Little Tokyo

King Cobra beat Mike Blood

Bull Ramos beat Chris Curtis

Bowyer had a reputation for getting job men to quit the business. Bowyer broke into wrestling in 1966 after being trained by
Verne Gagne and Eddie Sharkey. Like Billy Robinson and a few
other highly competent wrestlers and martial artists, Bowyer
sometimes had difficulty sticking to the script once inside the
ring. He was a shooter, and if his temper was up, was one to be
feared. Bowyer left the AWA in the late 1960s to live in Califor-
nia, then he headed to Kansas City. By 1979, he was working the
Mid-South circuit.

One Saturday morning, a guy came to the TV studio in
Shreveport and asked for a tryout. He was nice, very polite, and
wore a suit. An amateur wrestler, he'd been told that Watts was
the person to see about going pro. Watts put him up against
Ben Alexander, and the guy did pretty well. Next, he wrestled
Mike George and again acquitted himself well. Watts then put
him in the ring against a third opponent, Mike Bowyer. On the
side, Watts told Bowyer to stretch the guy. Now, the guy had just
worked two opponents, so he was tired. Bowyer easily got him
in a chokehold, then jabbed him in the rectum with his thumb.
Bowyer's move made the guy shit all over himself. We were all

sitting there watching. Even the Freebirds, the biggest heels in the business, were angry that Watts and Bowyer had humiliated someone like that. There was no reason for it.

Bowyer's formidable strength and his inability to control his temper led him into Watts's inner circle of trusted enforcers. They were guys who did the dirty work for Watts—maybe stretch a guy or punish him for some perceived insult. Bowyer was also a Jekyll and Hyde personality, so he was hard to read. The jobbers quickly learned it was better to stay on his good side because you never knew what to expect.

In the ring with Bowyer, I was doing my best to take his cues and sell for him, but the match wasn't going well, and I could tell Bowyer was getting angrier by the minute. Without warning, he hooked me in a front face lock, the same move Bruno Sammartino had used on Dr. Bill Miller, and applied full pressure. Bowyer signaled to the referee that I give up or else! I gave up immediately. I went to the dressing room angry with Bowyer for the dirty trick he pulled and angry with myself for not doing a better job of putting him over. Suddenly, Bowyer came over to me, looking like he was going to finish me off once and for all. I readied myself for a dressing room beatdown, but to his credit, Bowyer calmed down. He yelled at me for a few minutes, then pointed out some of the cues I missed and things I could do to improve my performances in the future. I think the other guys in the dressing room were stunned that no one had to call an ambulance! Then Bowyer showed me how to apply the front face lock for real in case I ever had to choke someone out. Bowyer was always nice to me after that. In fact, I wrestled him on my last night with Mid-South Wrestling. It was a great match and seemed like a good way to leave Bill Watts.

I left Louisiana in March 1980 to return to Milwaukee and the AWA. The Louisiana territory was thinning out and couldn't support all the job men in it. I think the Mid-South went to small towns too often and oversaturated their markets. In retrospect, it would have been a better idea to perform in each town twice a month or maybe even once every three weeks. When attendance went down, promoters found they had too many job men on their hands. I offered to leave because I really wasn't crazy about working for Bill Watts. I called Wally Karbo, and he said he would be happy to have me back. The Peter Szabo incident had been forgotten, and nobody held any grudges against me. I packed up the few things I had in Baton Rouge and turned the apartment over to Apache Bull Ramos, who'd been splitting the rent with me for two months. As I drove fifteen hundred miles back to Wisconsin, I reflected on my time with Watts on the Mid-South circuit. I was returning to the AWA a much more seasoned wrestler than I'd been six months earlier, and I was eager to apply my new skills to matches with old friends.

I found an apartment on Oakland Avenue in Milwaukee and began reestablishing contact with people who could give me work. In addition to steady gigs from the AWA, I was wrestling on the side at Federation Hall for twenty dollars a night. And whenever I could get four or five guys to share the cost of transportation, I worked outlaw shows in Indiana and Illinois. Sometimes when I worked an outlaw, I wrestled as Beautiful Bruce Swayze and hailed from San Francisco, just to stay under the AWA's radar. Outlaw shows operated at county fairs, high schools, firemen's picnics, church festivals—in short, just about any place where a promoter could set up a ring and put on a card. The pay wasn't great, but the work kept me in shape and allowed me to practice moves and holds that I wouldn't use during AWA matches. By the following year, I didn't have time to do as many independent cards because I was getting more AWA house shows in Milwaukee, Green Bay, and Rockford. Those gigs paid $150 plus expenses. Supplementing my income were the frequent TV matches I taped at $100 each.

I loved doing the TV tapings because funny stuff always happened. For instance, Blackjack Lanza had begun helping Karbo book jobbers for TV. Lanza had me come to St. Paul one evening to tape some matches. He also booked four guys from Iowa who worked for Bob Geigel in the Kansas City office. One of the Iowa jobbers was a police officer who wrestled as a babyface. His tag team match was terrible, and so was he. And his partner wasn't much better. When they got back to the dressing room, Verne Gagne was waiting for them, madder than a wet hen.

Gagne tore both guys a new one, demanding to know where they had worked previously. The cop told Gagne they worked for Geigel. Gagne was speechless. He was trying to process how Bob Geigel would have had anyone who performed that badly in the ring working for him. I found myself wondering the same thing. But it didn't matter, because I knew what was coming next!

Gagne's temper went from zero to sixty in the blink of an eye. "How the fuck can you guys call yourselves wrestlers?" he screamed. "What do I have to do to get somebody in here who can work?" The cop responded in kind. He got in Gagne's face and said, "You can't talk to me like that, I'm a police officer!" That *really* lit Gagne's fuse. He screamed at the cop, "I don't give a shit what you are. I don't care if you have your gun and badge on you. This is *my* show, and if you don't leave right now, I'll kick your ass good!" That sent the guys from Iowa running out. Then Gagne turned to Lanza and asked, "Who the fuck booked these guys? Did you, Jack?" Lanza was petrified. He told Gagne, "No, Wally booked 'em." Gagne started yelling, "Goddamn it, where's Wally?" I had to turn around and walk away because I was laughing so hard. One, Lanza had indeed booked those guys, and two, Karbo wasn't even at the taping.

In July 1981, Karbo hired me to work Olympic wrestler Laurent Soucie at the St. Paul Civic Center. Soucie was new to the business, and we had never met, but since he lived in Milwaukee,

MARCH 9, 1980, MINNEAPOLIS TV

Dino Bravo beat Ricky Hunter

Super Destroyer Mark II beat Herman Schaefer

Jerry Blackwell beat Ron Ritchie

Adrian Adonis and Jesse Ventura beat Chris Curtis and
Tony Leone

MARCH 30, 1980, MINNEAPOLIS TV

Buck Zumhofe beat George Allen

Adrian Adonis and Jesse Ventura beat Juan Valez and
Cesar Pabón

Super Destroyer Mark III beat Chris Curtis

Jerry Blackwell beat Herman Schaefer

Super Destroyer Mark II beat Armando Rodriguez

APRIL 12, 1980, BOYLAN HIGH SCHOOL—
ROCKFORD, ILLINOIS

Greg Gagne beat AWA champion Nick Bockwinkel

Super Destroyer Mark II and Bobby Heenan beat
Super Destroyer Mark III and Lord Alfred Hayes

APRIL 13, 1980, FEDERATION HALL—
MILWAUKEE, WISCONSIN

Jake LeCor vs. Jeff Jakubiak

Don Haack and Mystery Partner beat Beautiful Buford and
Bruce Swayze

Tank Roundhurst vs. the Masked Enforcer

Dallas Young vs. Red Allen

Lee Dalton vs. Bobby Mendocino

MAY 11, 1980, MINNEAPOLIS TV

Dino Bravo beat Chris Curtis
Adrian Adonis and Jesse Ventura beat Larry Powers and
    Mark Dartell
Steve Olsonoski beat Ben Deleon
Jerry Blackwell beat Armando Rodriguez
Super Destroyer Mark II beat Dick Young

**AUGUST 17, 1980, FEDERATION HALL—
MILWAUKEE, WISCONSIN**

Bruce Swayze beat Dallas Young

**DECEMBER 14, 1980, FEDERATION HALL—
MILWAUKEE, WISCONSIN**

Big Will Hagan won a fourteen-man battle royal
Bruce Swayze beat Tompall Mendocino (DQ)
Jeff Jakubiak beat Little Beaver
Ed Hibl drew Red Allen
Dan Diamond beat Hank Roundhurst
Beuford Butt drew Dallas Young
The Enforcer beat Len Atlas

**FEBRUARY 15, 1981, FEDERATION HALL—
MILWAUKEE, WISCONSIN**

Tompaul Mendocino and Drew Richards beat
    Bobby Mendocino and Bruce Swayze

APRIL 12, 1981, MINNEAPOLIS TV

Jim Brunzell beat Billy Howard
Jerry Blackwell and John Studd beat George Gadaski and
    Kenny Jay
Tito Santana beat Ben Deleon
Adrian Adonis beat Art Santos
Buck Zumhofe beat Chris Curtis

APRIL 19, 1981, MINNEAPOLIS TV

Greg Gagne and Jim Brunzell beat Steve Regal and
  Billy Howard
Jesse Ventura beat Art Santos
Tito Santana beat Chris Curtis
Jerry Blackwell beat Ben Deleon
Buck Zumhofe beat Tony Leone

**JUNE 14, 1981, BROWN COUNTY VETERANS
MEMORIAL ARENA—GREEN BAY, WISCONSIN**

Greg Gagne and Jim Brunzell beat Adrian Adonis and
  Jesse Ventura to win AWA tag team title
Baron von Raschke vs. Jerry Blackwell (double
  disqualification [DDQ])
AWA light heavyweight champion Mike Graham beat
  Buck Zumhofe
Laurent Soucie beat Ben DeLeon
George Gadaski beat Tony Leone
Brad Rheingans beat Chris Curtis

**JUNE 20, 1981, BOYLAN HIGH SCHOOL—
ROCKFORD, ILLINOIS**

AWA champion Nick Bockwinkel beat Jim Brunzell
Tito Santana beat Sheik Adnan Al-Kaissie (DQ)
Baron von Raschke beat Bobby Heenan
Ray Stevens beat Ben DeLeon
Buck Zumhofe beat Chris Curtis

**JULY 18, 1981, BOYLAN HIGH SCHOOL—
ROCKFORD, ILLINOIS**

AWA champion Nick Bockwinkel vs. Jim Brunzell (NC)
Jerry Blackwell beat Brad Rheingans
Jerry Blackwell beat Chris Curtis
Laurent Soucie beat Tony Leone

we decided to drive up together. About halfway there he asked if we could stop at a wayside and work on our match. We found some grass and started practicing wrestling holds and flips. People driving through stared at us. Practicing a little bit together before we got to St. Paul seemed like a good idea, but that evening's match against Soucie in the Civic Center was one of the worst experiences of my life!

To this day, I don't know what happened. Soucie and I went over the opening, the high spots, and the finish in the dressing room. When we got in the ring, Soucie couldn't remember a thing. He didn't respond to any of my cues, and it seemed like he couldn't hear anything I said to him. Once again, as luck would have it, Karbo stopped in that night and happened to catch our bout. "Jesus, Curtis, what happened out there?" Karbo asked. You notice how nobody ever asks the other guy what happened? No, it's always on Curtis! I said, "Wally, we went over it in the dressing room, and Soucie just didn't get it. I don't know anything more than that." It was odd, especially because Soucie was an excellent wrestler. He's in the Wisconsin High School Wrestling Hall of Fame and was an alternate member of the 1976 US Olympic team. When Soucie first went pro, Verne Gagne sent him to the Carolina territory to learn the ropes. The office down there was run by Ole Anderson. During the drive to our match in St. Paul, Soucie told me when he went to work for Anderson, a couple of jobbers from the office drove him to a high school football stadium and made him run the bleachers for a few hours. When they came back, Anderson told a couple of his shooters to stretch Soucie in some exhibition matches. Soucie figured out pretty quickly what was happening, and he stretched Anderson's guys instead! Furious, Anderson called Gagne and asked him what the hell was going on. Gagne just said, "Oh, didn't I tell you Soucie was on the Olympic team?"

A week after I wrestled Soucie, Karbo called with a job at

One of my best matches was against Laurent Soucie in July 1981.
LARRY WIDEN

the International Amphitheatre in Chicago. "You'll be working for Bruiser," he said, "and by the way, you got Laurent Soucie again." "What!" I yelled, "Wally, are you kidding me? After what happened in St. Paul?" I think they sent me down there to give Soucie more experience. To my surprise, it was one of the greatest

JULY 19, 1981, ST. PAUL CIVIC CENTER— ST. PAUL, MINNESOTA

AWA tag team champions Greg Gagne and Jim Brunzell
    beat Adrian Adonis and Jesse Ventura
Sheik Adnan Al-Kaissie beat Tito Santana (counted out of
    the ring [COR])
Jerry Blackwell beat Brad Rheingans
Baron von Raschke beat Ben DeLeon
Buck Zumhofe beat George Gadaski
Laurent Soucie beat Chris Curtis

matches I ever had. Soucie got everything right. All the falls, the high spots, the heat, the comeback, it was all fantastic. Even better, the crowd loved it and really responded.

Looking back, I have to say that I think Soucie and I jinxed our match in St. Paul by over-rehearsing. After we bombed, I avoided choreographing my matches in too much detail, preferring to keep it simple. I began setting the matches by calling one high spot and the finish. The rest of it got worked out in the ring. Doing so left room to improvise, to see how the crowd was reacting. For the Soucie match in Chicago, I baited the crowd by turning my back on the flag during the national anthem. Since Soucie had represented the United States at the Olympics, I ticked the fans off by disrespecting the flag! All the booing I caught eventually brought my girlfriend, who was in the stands to watch me wrestle for the first time, to tears. And it didn't help that the guy sitting next to her was calling me every name in the book. After I told her how things work in professional wrestling, she felt better when she understood it was my job to get the crowd to hate me.

That September, I got a TV match against Hulk Hogan. By the fall of 1981, Hogan was one of the biggest draws in professional

JULY 18, 1981, BOYLAN HIGH SCHOOL— ROCKFORD, ILLINOIS

AWA champion Nick Bockwinkel vs. Jim Brunzell (NC)
Jerry Blackwell beat Chris Curtis
Laurent Soucie beat Tony Leone

AUGUST 1, 1981, MILWAUKEE AUDITORIUM— MILWAUKEE, WISCONSIN

Adrian Adonis and Jesse Ventura beat AWA tag team
    champions Greg Gagne and Jim Brunzell
Baron von Raschke vs. Sheik Adnan Al-Kaissie (DDQ)
Hulk Hogan beat Tony Leone and Chuck Greenlee
Evan Johnson beat Chris Curtis
Laurent Soucie beat Nacho Berrara

AUGUST 15, 1981, BOYLAN HIGH SCHOOL— ROCKFORD, ILLINOIS

AWA tag team champions Greg Gagne and Jim Brunzell
    beat Adrian Adonis and Jesse Ventura
Tito Santana beat Sheik Adnan Al-Kaissie (DQ)
Hulk Hogan beat Ed Boulder, Chris Curtis, and Tony Leone
Brad Rheingans beat Ben DeLeon
George Gadaski beat Nacho Barrera

AUGUST 30, 1981, MINNEAPOLIS TV

Tito Santana beat Herman Schaefer
Nick Bockwinkel beat Tony Leone
Hulk Hogan beat Fred Torres
Greg Gagne and Jim Brunzell beat Chris Curtis and
    Tom Stone
Ed Boulder beat Terry Scholes

wrestling. When I wrestled him, he had just finished filming *Rocky III* with Sylvester Stallone. Hogan broke into the business in 1976 after training with Hiro Matsuda, the Japanese shooter and submission wrestler, who broke Hogan's leg. Two months later, Hogan came back and resumed training with Matsuda. He said Matsuda broke his leg on purpose to see if he had what it took to come back. Hogan wrestled Brian Blair in Fort Myers, Florida, in August 1977, and after that, he worked the Tennessee and Alabama territories. In 1979, Vince McMahon Sr. brought him to the WWF and gave him the name "Hulk." Helped by his manager, Fred Blassie, Hogan quickly became a top heel. After a year of being bossed around by McMahon, Hogan moved to the AWA and used "Luscious" Johnny Valiant as his manager. The fans loved Hogan, and Verne Gagne turned him from a heel to a babyface in a hurry. I wrestled Hogan a number of times from 1981 to 1983, and I have to say he was the lightest worker I ever had in the ring. It was like throwing a three-hundred-pound feather around in there. More important, Hogan was really a decent guy. He took care of everyone he wrestled to see they didn't get hurt. I could have wrestled a guy like Hulk Hogan every night for a year.

Another interesting thing happened that September. Remember how I said I'd drop whatever I was doing if the office called with a job? Well, my never-say-no policy caused a bit of friction

---

SEPTEMBER 6, 1981, MINNEAPOLIS TV

Billy Robinson beat Herman Schaefer

Adrian Adonis and Jesse Ventura beat Tony Leone and
    Terry Scholes

Hulk Hogan beat Chris Curtis

Sheik Adnan Al-Kaissie beat Fred Torres

Jerry Blackwell beat Tom Stone

Working against Hulk Hogan. He was always a professional and a gentleman.
LARRY WHITTIW

in my family because I accepted a match on September 12 against Buck Zumhofe in Milwaukee. Unfortunately, my sister Cindy (yes, the same one I threw the ball at) was getting married on September 12, and I was standing up in the wedding. Zumhofe was doing interviews on television promoting the match at least two weeks before we were going to wrestle. There was no getting out of it, so I went to my mom and said, "I have to wrestle on Saturday. How am I going to work this out?" Mom said, "It's simple. You can't wrestle. Your sister's getting married. Call the office and tell them you can't do it." Right. Like *that's* going to happen. Things got worse when an ad in the Thursday paper listed my match with Zumhofe.

My sister went ballistic when she saw the ad. After she calmed down, I told her how I thought it could work. I didn't have to be at the Milwaukee Auditorium until seven thirty in the evening, so standing up in the wedding party and being at the head

SEPTEMBER 12, 1981, MILWAUKEE
AUDITORIUM—MILWAUKEE, WISCONSIN

Sheik Adnan Al-Kaissie beat AWA champion
  Nick Bockwinkel (DQ)
Hulk Hogan beat Jerry Blackwell (COR)
Tito Santana and Buck Zumhofe beat Bobby Heenan and
  Ray Stevens
Evan Johnson beat Tony Leone
Ed Boulder beat Chris Curtis

table for dinner was no problem. Cindy agreed to postpone the
wedding dance until I got back. Right after dinner, I grabbed my
gym bag and raced down to the Milwaukee Auditorium from the
Tyrolean House banquet hall. I showed up in the dressing room
still wearing my tuxedo, which gave the guys a big laugh. When I
told them the story, Ray Stevens said, "Wow, I can't believe you
got away with this." Nick Bockwinkel was holding all the finishes
and said, "I have an idea. Instead of wrestling Buck, I'll put you
on first against Boulder. Go eight minutes and get the hell out of
here!" Bockwinkel always liked me, and he did me a big favor that
night. He took Ed Boulder out of the tag match with Stevens and
Bobby Heenan and replaced him with Buck.

Once Boulder pinned me, I showered, put my tux on, and
high-tailed it back to the Tyrolean House. I had been gone less
than ninety minutes! I was hardly missed, and the wedding dance
went off without a hitch.

A few days after my sister's wedding, I got a call from Mar-
lene Widen, Larry Widen's mom, asking if I could help her with
a community service project. Mrs. Widen was a mental health
counselor, and she had placed some men in a group home on

the northwest side of Milwaukee. They suffered from a variety of mental health problems, such as schizophrenia, that prevented them from holding down jobs or engaging in typical daily routines. But those guys loved wrestling, and Mrs. Widen thought it would be good therapy for them to talk to someone in the business. Too bad the only person she could think to call was me! Still, I said I'd give it a try. It turned out to be really fun. The guys asked me a million questions and loved hearing stories about wrestlers and matches. I probably didn't tell them anything they didn't already know, given that they were such big fans. I spent all afternoon with them, and I probably could have stayed longer, but Mrs. Widen said we had to go. I'm glad I could do something for those men. Sometimes I think about them and wonder where they are and what they are doing.

SEPTEMBER 20, 1981, MINNEAPOLIS TV

Baron von Raschke beat Tom Stone
Hulk Hogan beat Chris Curtis
Jerry Blackwell beat Rick Young
Greg Gagne and Jim Brunzell beat Herman Schaefer and
    Nacho Berrera
Sheik Adnan Al-Kaissie beat Sonny Rogers

DECEMBER 6, 1981, MINNEAPOLIS TV

Jim Brunzell beat Tom Stone
Hulk Hogan beat Chris Curtis and Jake Milliman
Evan Johnson beat Herman Schaefer
Sheik Adnan Al-Kaissie beat Chuck Greenlee
Tito Santana and Buck Zumhofe vs. Ken Patera and
    Bobby Duncum (NC)

DECEMBER 27, 1981, MINNEAPOLIS TV

Hulk Hogan beat Tony Leone
Baron von Raschke beat Nacho Berrera
Sheik Adnan Al-Kaissie beat Terry Scholl
Brad Rheingans beat Chris Curtis
Ken Patera beat Tom Stone

JANUARY 3, 1982, MINNEAPOLIS TV

Tito Santana beat Fred Torres
Brad Rheingans beat Tom Stone
Buck Zumhofe beat Tony Leone
Evan Johnson beat Chris Curtis

FEBRUARY 14, 1982, MINNEAPOLIS TV

Bobby Duncum beat Ricky Hunter
Greg Gagne and Jim Brunzell beat Buddy Lane and
    Chris Curtis
Sheik Adnan Al-Kaissie beat Jake Milliman
Tito Santana beat Woody Wilson
Brad Rheingans beat Kenny Jay

FEBRUARY 21, 1982, MINNEAPOLIS TV

Hulk Hogan beat Woody Wilson and Chris Curtis
Bobby Duncum beat Buddy Lane
Baron von Raschke beat Jake Milliman
Brad Rheingans beat Ricky Hunter

MARCH 14, 1982, MINNEAPOLIS TV

Tito Santana beat Herman Schaefer
Jerry Blackwell and Sheik Adnan Al-Kaissie beat
    Sonny Rogers and Nacho Berrera
Greg Gagne beat Tom Stone

Ken Patera beat Chris Curtis
Buck Zumhofe beat Fred Torres

MARCH 21, 1982, MINNEAPOLIS TV

Bobby Duncum beat Tom Stone
Greg Gagne and Jim Brunzell beat Herman Schaefer and
  Chris Curtis
Sgt. Jacques Goulet beat Sonny Rogers
Baron von Raschke beat Fred Torres
Sheik Adnan Al-Kaissie beat Nacho Berrera

MAY 2, 1982, MINNEAPOLIS TV

Hulk Hogan beat Fred Torres
Pat Patterson and Ray Stevens beat Herman Schaefer and
  Tom Stone
Buck Zumhofe beat Chris Curtis
Sgt. Jacques Goulet beat Kenny Jay
Brad Rheingans beat Woody Wilson

MAY 9, 1982, MINNEAPOLIS TV

Jim Brunzell beat Woody Wilson
Jerry Blackwell and Sheik Adnan Al-Kaissie beat Kenny Jay
  and Tom Stone
Evan Johnson beat Chris Curtis
Pat Patterson beat Herman Schaefer
Baron von Raschke beat Fred Torres

MAY 30, 1982, MINNEAPOLIS TV

Nick Bockwinkel beat Chris Curtis
Brad Rheingans vs. Tony Leone
Ken Patera and Bobby Duncum vs. Tom Stone and
  Gonzo Gonzales

Baron von Raschke vs. Nacho Berrera
Sheik Adnan Al-Kaissie vs. Juan Sebastian

JUNE 6, 1982, MINNEAPOLIS TV

Greg Gagne beat Chris Curtis
Jerry Blackwell beat Nacho Berrera
Tito Santana beat Tony Leone
Sgt. Jacques Goulet beat Juan Sebastian

AUGUST 22, 1982, MINNEAPOLIS TV

Rick Martel beat Tom Stone
Bobby Duncum beat Jake Milliman
Greg Gagne and Jim Brunzell beat Tony Leone and
  Chris Curtis
Otto Wanz beat Woody Wilson
Ray Stevens beat Herman Schaefer

SEPTEMBER 26, 1982, MINNEAPOLIS TV

Jerry Blackwell and Sheik Adnan Al-Kaissie beat
  Buddy Lane and Al Snow
Rick Martel beat Chris Curtis
Sgt. Jacques Goulet beat Koko Lewis
Buck Zumhofe beat Ben Patrick
Curt Hennig beat Puppy Dog Peloquin

OCTOBER 3, 1982, MINNEAPOLIS TV

Jerry Blackwell beat Koko Lewis and Ben Patrick
Greg Gagne and Jim Brunzell beat Buddy Lane and
  Chris Curtis
Ken Patera beat Al Snow
Rick Martel beat Puppy Dog Peloquin
Baron von Raschke beat Woody Wilson

OCTOBER 16, 1982, SHEBOYGAN, WISCONSIN

Fifteen-man battle royal with Tom Stone, Buck Zumhofe,
Ray Stevens, Sgt. Jacques Goulet, Brad Rheingans,
Baron von Raschke, Otto Wanz, Ken Patera,
Bobby Heenan, Bobby Duncum, Jerry Blackwell,
Rick Martel, Sheik Adnan Al-Kaissie, Adrian Adonis,
and André the Giant
André the Giant vs. Jerry Blackwell
Adrian Adonis vs. Rick Martel
Baron von Raschke vs. Sheik Adnan Al-Kaissie
Ray Stevens beat Bobby Heenan (DQ)
Referees: Chris Curtis and Larry Lisowski

OCTOBER 24, 1982, MINNEAPOLIS TV

Steve Olsonoski and Rick Martel beat Herman Schaefer and
Ben Deleon
Sheik Adnan Al-Kaissie beat Chris Curtis
Brad Rheingans beat Tony Leone

**NOVEMBER 6, 1982, BRADFORD HIGH
SCHOOL—KENOSHA, WISCONSIN**

André the Giant won a fourteen-man battle royal with card
wrestlers and Ken Patera, Chris Curtis, Tom Stone,
Herman Schaefer, and Sheik Adnan Al-Kaissie
André the Giant beat Bobby Duncum
Jerry Blackwell beat Larry Hennig
Brad Rheingans beat Sgt. Jacques Goulet
Baron von Raschke beat Bobby Heenan

JANUARY 16, 1983, MINNEAPOLIS TV

Rick Martel beat Puppy Dog Peloquin
Hulk Hogan beat Chris Curtis

Ken Patera and Bobby Duncum beat Buddy Lane and
Sonny Rogers
Wahoo McDaniel beat Tony Leone

JULY 24, 1983, MINNEAPOLIS TV

Rick Martel beat Chris Curtis
Mr. Saito beat Buddy Lane
Ken Patera and Jerry Blackwell beat Puppy Dog Peloquin
and Tom Stone
David Shults beat Jake Milliman

JULY 31, 1983, MINNEAPOLIS TV

Bill White beat Puppy Dog Peloquin
Greg Gagne beat Chris Curtis
David Shults beat Buddy Lane
Wahoo McDaniel beat Tom Stone
Ken Patera beat Jake Milliman
Brad Rheingans beat Larry Jones

AUGUST 7, 1983, MINNEAPOLIS TV

Rick Martel and Tom Stone beat Ken Patera and
Jerry Blackwell (DQ)
Mr. Saito beat Jake Milliman
Baron von Raschke beat Chris Curtis
Bill White beat Larry Jones

AUGUST 21, 1983, MILWAUKEE AUDITORIUM—
MILWAUKEE, WISCONSIN

Mad Dog Vachon beat Jerry Blackwell
Hulk Hogan vs. David Shults (NC)
Greg Gagne beat Bill White
Jim Brunzell beat Sheik Adnan Al-Kaissie

Mr. Saito beat Steve Olsonoski
Baron von Raschke beat Blackjack Lanza
Referee: Chris Curtis

OCTOBER 16, 1983, MINNEAPOLIS TV

Rick Martel beat Chris Curtis
Mr. Saito and David Shults beat Stormy Granzig and
    Charles Young
Jerry Blackwell beat Ricky Anderson

NOVEMBER 6, 1983, MINNEAPOLIS TV

Sonny Rogers beat Bill White (DQ)
Billy Robinson beat Chris Curtis
Billy Graham beat Tony Leone
Hulk Hogan beat Tom Stone and Mike Richards

NOVEMBER 13, 1983, MINNEAPOLIS TV

Baron von Raschke beat Mike Richards
Mr. Saito beat Tom Stone
Hulk Hogan beat Tony Leone and Chris Curtis
Buck Zumhofe beat Bill White (DQ)

Chapter 6

Around 1982, I started to do a lot of refereeing for the AWA. I enjoyed refereeing because I was still in the ring, but my role wasn't
quite the same as when I was jobbing for the stars. One night in
Milwaukee, Nick Bockwinkel defended his title against Wahoo
McDaniel in the main event. The match ended in a no contest, but
playing to the crowd, McDaniel threw Bockwinkel out of the ring
and grabbed the belt. The crowd booed when I got in Wahoo's face
to remind him the title didn't change hands on disqualifications
and no-contest decisions. Then I threatened to take the matter to
AWA president Stanley Blackburn. McDaniel wasn't to be stopped.
He tore the belt from my hands and pushed me aside. As the crowd
roared their approval, McDaniel ran back to the dressing room
holding the belt over his head. I chased after him, and we started
scuffling at the back of the auditorium. When I took the belt from
him, Wahoo gave me a huge tomahawk chop on my forehead. I
sold the chop, flying backward and taking a fantastic bump right
on the concrete floor. I landed so hard that I split my pants wide
open at the crotch from front to back. While Wahoo dashed into
the dressing room, I continued to sell the bump, holding my torn
pants together and pretending like my back was killing me from
the fall. The crowd was in a frenzy as I staggered into the dressing
room. And McDaniel? He was already in the shower, laughing
about my torn trousers. The rest of the guys told Bockwinkel about
it, since he was still in the ring and missed most of the action. I still
think that was one of my best bumps ever.

Other crazy stuff happened when I was a referee. I refereed a bout in Milwaukee between Steve Olsonoski and Mr. Saito. Olsonoski was on his back, and Saito had Olsonoski's left leg in an ankle lock, going for a submission. I looked at Olsonoski to see if he'd tap out. He was making faces and smiling at me. The crowd couldn't see it because he had both forearms covering the sides of his face. Olsonoski kept making faces, and I was trying not to laugh. To cover up, I yelled out, asking if he wanted to give up. In a faint, effeminate voice, he said, "Yeah." I thought I was gonna burst out laughing at that point, so I tapped Saito on the shoulder and said, "Kill him."

Sometimes I had to get between fans and the talent. I was refereeing a match in Green Bay featuring Jerry Blackwell, and as Blackwell was walking back to the dressing room, a guy jumped into the aisle and hit Blackwell from behind. Blackwell turned around, and man was he upset. As quick as I could, I stepped between him and the fan while waving for the cops. The cops helped, but only a little. Instead of escorting the fan out, they brought him back to the dressing room and marched him up to Blackwell, saying, "He's all yours." Blackwell stood up and came at the guy, telling him, "You fucker, I'm gonna choke the living shit outta you." The fan did us all a big favor and fainted before Blackwell could lay a hand on him. I'm pretty sure Blackwell was just kidding around when the guy keeled over, but with him, you could never be 100 percent certain.

On another occasion, I refereed a great match between Bobby Duncum and Tito Santana. Bobby Heenan was in Duncum's corner, which guaranteed that some kind of interference or cheating was going to happen. As I climbed into the ring, I heard someone yell my name. I looked out in the crowd and saw Tina, a friend I'd known for a long time, sitting in the fifth row with her boyfriend. Tina was a huge wrestling fan and, in particular, was crazy about Tito Santana. I'm sure that thrilled her boyfriend. I waved at Tina,

**MAY 15, 1983, MILWAUKEE AUDITORIUM—
MILWAUKEE, WISCONSIN**

AWA champion Nick Bockwinkel beat Wahoo McDaniel
AWA tag team champions Greg Gagne and Jim Brunzell
    beat Jesse Ventura and Blackjack Lanza
Mad Dog Vachon beat Jerry Blackwell
Ken Patera beat Jerry Lawler
Baron von Raschke beat John Tolos
Buck Zumhofe beat Sgt. Jacques Goulet
Referee: Chris Curtis

and we got the match under way. During the finish, Santana was making his comeback and hit Duncum with a shoulder block. Duncum flew back and smashed into me, and I sold it with a big bump. Heenan held Santana's foot so Duncum could knock him out. Of course, I recovered from Duncum's hit just in time to see the pin and count Santana out. The crowd was furious at the outcome, but they weren't mad at Heenan. They were mad at *me* for not seeing Heenan's cheating! Yet what happened *after* the match was even better. Every time I saw Tina, she gave me the cold shoulder. She wouldn't speak to me for about three months because she thought my incompetence had cost her beloved Tito Santana the match! It was the price I paid for being good at my job. Being a referee is fun, but it's almost harder than wrestling. In order for the heel to get his heat, the referee has to be in the exact place at the right time, or the whole thing falls flat. If Duncum knows he's supposed to collide with me, and I'm not in the right position, he stumbles, or improvises, and chances are he looks like a fool—not unlike the time I wrestled Peter Szabo and he missed his cues.

My brother Tim, who was seventeen at the time, came up with me and watched from ringside as I refereed a title match between the Crusher and Bockwinkel. Heenan was in Bock-winkel's corner, and the finish was fantastic. When the Crusher started to make his comeback on Bockwinkel, Heenan jumped up on the ring apron to protest. The Crusher stopped working Bockwinkel and went over to get Heenan. My job was to make sure I was in between them so I could take the punch the Crusher intended for Heenan. At the same time, Heenan pulled brass knuckles out of his trunks and hurled them to Bockwinkel over the Crusher and myself. When I turned and yelled at Heenan, Bockwinkel hit the Crusher with the knuckles, and he went down like a sack of bricks. I looked around just in time to see Bockwinkel pin the Crusher. I counted him out and the match was over. The crowd was hysterical. They tried to attack Heenan and me on our way back to the dressing room. Thank God we had the Brown County Sheriff's Department there because I don't know how things would have turned out otherwise. There were about one hundred people in the parking lot waiting for us by our cars, and they were not there to congratulate us for anything. The sheriff took a look at the situation and said, "We have to walk you guys out there or those people are gonna take you apart." First, though, the sheriffs had to go down to the seats and get my brother so we could all leave at once. After the sheriffs escorted us to our cars, they followed us down Lombardi Avenue and made sure we got on the highway. I thought fans in Chicago were crazy about the Crusher, but they seemed pretty laid back in comparison to the fans in Green Bay.

What happened in Green Bay that night had happened to an even greater degree years earlier. On August 24, 1957, there was a riot following the main event at the Milwaukee Auditorium. Verne Gagne wrestled Boris and Nikolai Volkoff in front of 7,100 fans, with 2,000 people having been turned away. The Russian heels cheated, and the match ended in a brawl. People threw fruit, bottles, and even chairs into the ring. No one was hurt, and it wasn't all that big a deal, but it was the first time something like it had happened in Milwaukee. In response to some complaints, the Auditorium manager canceled the next three pro wrestling cards. At that time, the rental on the Auditorium for a Saturday night was $1,150 plus a percentage if the gate exceeded that figure. Money talks, and it wasn't long before the people who ran the Auditorium discovered that it was a lot cheaper to pay a few security guards than it was to lose rental income. Two years later, there was another crowd riot, this time at the Milwaukee Arena. Verne Gagne was again involved; as he and Hans Schmidt attacked each other with chairs, the fans went crazy. It took more than a dozen policemen to restore order. The Arena suspended pro wrestling cards again, this time for seven months. Wrestling wasn't allowed back in Milwaukee until March of 1960!

I think the funniest match I ever refereed was held at the University of Wisconsin–Eau Claire. It was one of those nights when, because I was the only referee, I had to run back and forth from the heel dressing room to the babyface dressing room to give the wrestlers their finishes. After doing that all night long, we got to the main event, which was Greg Gagne versus Sheik Adnan Al-Kaissie. Gagne gave me the finish and told me to give it to Adnan. On the way over to the other dressing room, I forgot what Gagne had told me! I wasn't about to go back and admit that I forgot what he had said to me, so I went to Adnan, who was putting on a gimmick cast from the time Verne Gagne supposedly broke his arm. I gave Adnan the match and told him I'd give him the finish when we were in the ring. He said, "Goddammit, you sonofabitch, give it to me now!" I said, "Don't worry; we've got plenty of time." As time was running down in the match, Adnan had Gagne by the hair. Adnan looked at me and said, "Okay, what do I do?" I still couldn't remember the finish, so I said, "Hit him with the cast!" Adnan did as he was told and hit Gagne in the head. Gagne went down, and I disqualified Adnan for using the cast! Gagne played along with it until we got back to the dressing room, then he turned to me and said, "What the fuck was that?" I said, "Beats me. Adnan forgot the finish even though I went over it twice with him." Gagne just shook his head and said, "Goddamn that asshole!" I was laughing because, for once, I came out on top.

Another story that comes to mind isn't so amusing. When I was a referee, I worked matches in which Ken Patera or Mr. Saito wrestled. Patera was a world-class weightlifter before transitioning to professional wrestling. He won a gold medal at the 1971 Pan American Games, and a year later, he became the first American ever to clean and jerk five hundred pounds over his head. Verne Gagne called Patera in 1973 and invited him to Gagne's AWA wrestling camp outside of Minneapolis. Patera made it through the camp's grueling regime, then Verne sent him to Japan to perfect his ring persona. When Patera returned a year later, Gagne billed him as "The World's Strongest Man." As a heel, Patera was voted "Most Hated Wrestler" in 1977.

Like Patera, Masa Saito was also an accomplished athlete. A classically trained Japanese wrestler, Saito wrestled for Japan at the 1964 Olympics before turning pro in 1965. As Mr. Saito, he quickly established himself as a dangerous opponent in both Japan and the United States. Nicknamed "Mr. Torture" for his punishing and sadistic style, Saito was brutal in the ring and held a number of championship titles during his career. He gained international fame when in 1987 he wrestled arch rival Antonio Anoki on a deserted Japanese island in a match that lasted over two hours. The two agreed to end their blood lust for one another with a match on Ganryujima Island, a location revered in Japanese culture. In 1612, two famous swordsmen, Kojiro Sasaki and Musashi Miyamoto, fought a duel there that became so famous that the island remained a sacred place hundreds of years later. Anoki played off of the legend by thrusting Saito and himself into the roles of the swordsmen.

The wrestling careers of Ken Patera and Mr. Saito went off course one night while they were driving to Green Bay from a house show in Watertown. After deciding to stay overnight in Waukesha, Patera and Saito went to a nearby McDonald's to get dinner. When they pulled into the drive-thru, they were told the restaurant had already closed for the evening. Patera offered the attendant fifty dollars to serve him and Saito, explaining they were really hungry and they would take anything left over. The woman countered that all the ovens and fryers had been cleaned and shut down, so cooking food was not possible. Her refusal made Patera so angry that he roared out of the drive-thru and slammed on the brakes near the front of the restaurant. He got out of the car, picked up a huge boulder, and hurled it through a plate glass window in retaliation. The police were called and a brawl ensued. When one of the female officers struck Mr. Saito with her nightstick, he threw her across the parking lot, breaking her arm. Ultimately, it took thirteen police officers to subdue the wrestlers and place them under arrest. After a Waukesha County jury found both men guilty of battery and criminal damage to property, Patera served a two-year sentence at the maximum-security Waupun Correctional Institution. Saito served his time in a Wisconsin prison near Lac du Flambeau.

I witnessed Saito's hot temper in action one night in Green

**APRIL 5, 1984, WATERTOWN HIGH SCHOOL—
WATERTOWN, WISCONSIN**

The Crusher beat Mr. Saito

Blackjack Mulligan beat Ken Patera

The Fabulous Ones beat Steve Regal and Larry Zbyszko

Brad Rheingans beat Tom Stone

Kevin Kelly beat Buck Zumhofe

Bay. I was refereeing a six-man tag team match. The Crusher and the Fabulous Ones squared off against Mr. Saito, Nick Bockwinkel, and Steve Regal. At one point, the Crusher threw Saito over the top rope, and he landed on the floor. As Saito attempted to get back in the ring, a fan hit Saito in the back with a camera. Regal said to me, "Can you believe this idiot? He has no idea what Saito is capable of." Sure enough, Saito advanced on the fan. I yelled at him to stop. At the same time, I waved the cops over and pointed the guy out, screaming, "Get him out of here, now!" The cops marched the guy out of the arena, and to this day, I wonder if he knows the kind of beating I saved him from taking.

At the same time I was refereeing for the AWA, things were happening for me outside the ring as well. I got married in May 1984. My new wife, Janice, didn't know much about wrestling and was never told that matches were partly scripted. I didn't tell Janice how matches worked because I was protecting the business. Then I realized that when you're married, you shouldn't keep any secrets from your spouse. Or so I thought. Right after I got married, I received a call from Minneapolis to come in for TV. After I hung up, Janice said, "Why do you wrestle? I mean, it's dumb." When I asked why she'd say that, her response was, "Because you beat each other up." I said we only pretend to beat each other up. That didn't improve wrestling much in her estimation, and she replied, "Well, that's even dumber!" I went to Minneapolis thinking my marriage was going to be a very interesting relationship.

Eventually, I told Jan how some matches were done. I made her swear to secrecy for fear of catching hell from Verne Gagne or losing my job. After this, one night I was scheduled to wrestle Dallas Young in a chain match at Federation Hall. I told Jan I might have to do a blade job on myself to put the match over. Jan had a lot to say about that, but the short version is that she said, "If you do that, I'm leaving you." Jan made me promise before I left that I wouldn't do it. I said, "I promise." *Right.* During my match with Young, I had a blade taped to my index finger. When Dallas smacked me with the chain, I went down, holding my head with both hands. I nicked my scalp about an inch behind my hairline and the blood started flowing like crazy. After the match, I cleaned up and went home. Jan met me at the door, asking if I had kept my promise. Because the cut was behind my hairline, I slicked my hair back from my forehead and said, "See. No cuts!"

Jan never really understood why I wrestled for a living. As time went by, I found it interesting to see how women I dated reacted when they learned more about my career. The first thing they'd usually ask was, "Is it real?" My answer was always, "Do you think it is?" One woman, Heidi, replied, "Well, I thought they were really mad at each other because of the way they talk on TV!" Another woman I dated, Linda, thought professional wrestlers had to take some kind of oath and keep it secret. Well, there was no oath, but we all knew that if management found out

My ex-wife made me promise to stop doing blade jobs during my matches. After that, I kept my word (mostly). LARRY WIDEN

JUNE 9, 1984, MILWAUKEE AUDITORIUM—
MILWAUKEE, WISCONSIN

Baron von Raschke (representing the Crusher) sat chained
   to Abdullah the Butcher (representing Jerry Blackwell)
The Crusher beat Jerry Blackwell (DQ)
Steve Keirn beat Nick Bockwinkel (DQ)
Baron von Raschke beat Abdullah the Butcher (DQ)
The Fabulous Ones beat Larry Zbyszko and Steve Regal
King Kong Brody beat Steve Olsonoski
Tom Stone beat Jake Milliman
Referees: Larry Lisowski, Chris Curtis

a wrestler had been talking, that wrestler would be stretched by a shooter or a hook artist. Like a shooter, a hook artist, or hooker, specialized in submission holds skillfully applied to joints at the elbow, knee, or neck. Promoters kept a few hookers around to protect their businesses. When I wrestled, wrestlers kept their mouths shut or paid the price.

In the same year I married Janice, Vince McMahon Jr., owner of New York's World Wrestling Federation (WWF), made some aggressive business moves that ultimately damaged and forever changed the landscape of professional wrestling. When McMahon put on matches in the Midwest, first in St. Louis and then in Minneapolis, he insulted Pat O'Connor and Verne Gagne by doing so. McMahon threw aside any respect for territorial boundaries, violating business agreements that had been in place for decades.

Regardless, I was curious about the WWF. I got the chance to see it for myself when Steve Hall called me on June 16 and said, "Hey, New York needs a guy for tomorrow in Minneapolis. You want it?" I asked Hall if he was working the match as well. He said,

"No way. Gagne would kill me if I did." I wanted to take the job, not only because I wanted to know what it was like to wrestle in the WWF but also because the WWF paid so well. I called Hall back and told him I was in. He put me in touch with Red Bastein, who was booking job men for McMahon.

I flew to the Twin Cities the next day. When I got there, I learned I was wrestling Jesse Ventura, who had recently defected from Verne Gagne's operation to go with McMahon. Others had made the same move, including Mad Dog Vachon, Hulk Hogan, and Adrian Adonis. They told me they did it because the money McMahon offered was too good to pass up and that the WWF was the future of professional wrestling. I didn't like the sound of that, but I liked how I was treated that day. Even better, I was paid in cash on the spot. As for the match, for some reason, Ventura was pretty stiff that night.

Ventura may have been in good shape, but he wasn't a good wrestler. His real name is James Janos, and he was on the Navy's Underwater Demolition Team during the Vietnam War. In 1975, he broke into pro wrestling as Jesse "the Body" Ventura working for Bob Geigel's Central States Wrestling. When Ventura moved to the AWA in 1979, Gagne teamed him with another heel, Adrian Adonis, and called them the East-West Connection. They won the tag team championship belts from Gagne and Mad Dog Vachon a year later. I had worked Adonis and Ventura twice in tag team matches before the WWF hired me to wrestle Ventura in Minneapolis.

Now, just because Ventura wasn't any good in the ring doesn't mean he couldn't star doing other things. Ventura's real gift is his huge, larger-than-life personality. He could talk with the best of them, and his interviews and ringside commentaries with Gorilla Monsoon and Vince McMahon Jr. were second to none. It's no surprise that Jesse capitalized on his abilities and exposure, moving on from professional wrestling to become a successful author, actor, television show host, and the thirty-eighth governor of Minnesota.

My time in the WWF did not go unnoticed. Wally Karbo called when I returned from Minneapolis and asked me to do TV for the AWA the following weekend. When I got to the station for the taping, Verne Gagne took me aside and asked me how things had gone with the WWF. Gagne was a real gentleman, saying, "I'm glad you tried it to see how they did things, but I'd prefer if you'd work exclusively for us." For the next three years, that's exactly what I did.

It wasn't hard for me to stay with Gagne at the AWA. For one thing, I loved doing Minneapolis TV because I got to hang out with some of my favorite wrestlers. Additionally, as I've already said, funny stuff always happened when we were filming. A particularly hilarious and memorable moment occurred once when Paul Ellering was taping an interview at WTCN in Minneapolis. Ringside announcers Marty O'Neill and Rodger Kent conducted the interviews as a way to help sell tickets for house shows. Ellering was telling Kent how hard he was going try to beat his opponent, Jesse Ventura. While Ellering was talking, Pat Patterson crept underneath the camera right in front of Ellering. Patterson

JUNE 17, 1984, MET CENTER—MINNEAPOLIS, MINNESOTA

$50,000 eighteen-man battle royal: Big John Studd defeats Adrian Adonis, Alexis Smirnoff, André the Giant, B. Brian Blair, Chris Curtis, Dick Murdoch, Ivan Putski, Jerry Valiant, Jesse Ventura, Mil Mascaras, Mr. Fuji, Paul Orndorff, Sgt. Jacques Goulet, Rocky Johnson, Tiger Chung Lee, Tito Santana, and Tony Garea
Jesse Ventura beat Chris Curtis

had his shirt off and was sticking his beer belly way out, trying to make Ellering laugh. Standing nearby was Ray Stevens, his hand in a bucket of chicken. At that moment, Bobby Heenan and Verne Gagne walked in. Gagne looked at Stevens gobbling fried chicken and Patterson clowning under the camera, and asked, "What in the hell is going on?" Heenan told Gagne, "Those are your world tag team champions." Verne just shook his head and walked away. What else was he going to do? Stevens and Patterson were two of the best workers in the business.

Not long after Gagne asked me to stay with the AWA, he began giving me a lot of extra work. I was needed because Gagne had made a deal with the television network ESPN to create a monthly wrestling program broadcast from the Showboat Sports Pavilion in Las Vegas, Nevada. Gagne knew the business was changing and that he needed to do something like the Las Vegas show to stay in the game. Gagne was an old-school guy accustomed to doing shows the same way for twenty-five years, and he deserves credit for trying to adapt. Regional promoters like Gagne knew that Vince McMahon Jr. had thrown a curveball into the business of professional wrestling and that they needed to do whatever they could to grab what was left of the pie.

I loved doing the Las Vegas matches because the AWA flew me out there and put me up in the Showboat Hotel. Over the next few years, I wrestled Wahoo McDaniel, Brad Rheingans, Jerry "the King" Lawler, Cousin Luke, Jeff Jarrett, and Larry Zbyszko in Las Vegas. I also wrestled tag teams such as Doug Somers and Buddy Rose, the Rockers (Marty Jannetty and Shawn Michaels), and the Russians (Alexis Smirnoff and Yuri Gordienko). I even had an arm-wrestling contest with Kevin Kelly.

When I wasn't working in Las Vegas, I taped a lot of regional TV matches for the AWA at various locations across the Midwest. Gagne had started taping house shows held in high school or college gymnasiums rather than expensive civic auditoriums or arenas. His strategy accomplished two things. Gagne was able to boost sagging attendance at the house shows while eliminating the expense of renting the TV station in Minneapolis formerly used for taping. Plus, audiences had been able to watch wrestling at the TV studio for free, whereas attendees had to buy tickets for the house shows. Crowds got to see fifteen matches during a three-hour show, so the audience got their money's worth. I also liked the new system because I usually taped three matches in one night and got paid for each.

Now comes the moment you've all been waiting for: Chris Curtis finally wins a match! Even better, I won a title bout against world heavyweight champion Rick Martel. Why, then, am I not pictured in this book wearing the title belt? Well, there's a bit more to the story.

On October 26, 1985, it was my job to escalate a running angle

Heading back to the dressing room after a tough match. I gave everything I had every time I stepped into the ring.
LARRY WIDEN

between Martel and Stan Hansen. While Martel and I were going at it in the ring, Hansen came out of the dressing room and started taunting Martel from the ringside announcer's table. Greg Gagne, who was doing some color for the broadcast, told Hansen to knock it off. Hansen kept it up anyway, and finally Martel got out of the ring to deal with him. Referee Marty Miller counted Martel out, and I was declared the winner of the match. Miller raised my arm in victory and started to say, "And new heavyweight champ," but Gagne began yelling that the belt couldn't change hands on anything but a legitimate decision. I threw a few parting shots to Gagne and stomped around the ring a little before heading off to the showers. I was the AWA champ for about fifteen seconds, and it felt great!

JANUARY 11, 1986, BOYLAN HIGH SCHOOL— ROCKFORD, ILLINOIS

Jerry Blackwell and Scott Hall beat AWA tag team
 champions Jim Garvin and Steve Regal (DQ)
Nord the Barbarian, Mongolian Stomper, and Boris Zhukov
 beat Marty Jannetty, Buck Zumhofe, and Curt Hennig
Scott Irwin beat Baron von Raschke (DQ)
Larry Zbyszko beat Nick Bockwinkel
Sgt. Slaughter vs. Boris Zhukov (NC)
Jake Milliman beat Larry Zbyszko
Kelly Kiniski beat Scott Ferris
Stan Hansen beat Mike Richards
Marty Jannetty beat Chris Curtis
Nord the Barbarian and Mongolian Stomper beat
 Jake Milliman and Rick Gantner
Scott Hall beat Woody Wilson
Stan Hansen beat Chuck Greenlee

Jerry Blackwell beat Spike Jones
Bill Irwin and Scott Irwin beat the Alaskans
Marty Jannetty beat Rick Gantner
Nord the Barbarian beat Woody Wilson

JANUARY 24, 1986, STEVENS POINT, WISCONSIN

Boris Zhukov and Sheik Adnan Al-Kaissie beat Woody
    Wilson and Earthquake Ferris
AWA champion Stan Hansen beat Chris Curtis
Nord the Barbarian beat Mike Richards
AWA tag team champions Scott Hall and Curt Hennig beat
    Spike Jones and Doug Somers
Buck Zumhofe beat Chris Bassett
Scott Hall beat Chris Curtis
Scott Irwin and Bill Irwin beat Chris Bassett and
    Earthquake Ferris
Jimmy Garvin beat Woody Wilson
Sgt. Slaughter, Jerry Blackwell, and Curt Hennig
    drew Boris Zhukov, Nord the Barbarian, and
    Mongolian Stomper
Sgt. Slaughter beat Doug Somers
Larry Zbyszko beat Woody Wilson
Jimmy Garvin beat Chris Bassett
AWA champion Stan Hansen beat Spike Jones
Nick Bockwinkel beat Larry Zbyszko
Bill Irwin and Scott Irwin beat AWA tag team champions
    Scott Hall and Curt Hennig

FEBRUARY 1, 1986, OSHKOSH, WISCONSIN, TV

Jerry Blackwell vs. King Kong Brody (NC)
AWA champion Stan Hansen beat Curt Hennig (DQ)
Scott Hall beat Doug Somers

Curt Hennig, Jerry Blackwell, and Sgt. Slaughter beat
  Nord the Barbarian, Mongolian Stomper, and
  Boris Zhukov (DQ)
Leon White and Buck Zumhofe beat the Alaskans
Marty Jannetty beat Jake Milliman
Leon White beat Chris Curtis
King Kong Brody beat Mike Richards
Sgt. Slaughter beat Rick Gantner
Marty Jannetty beat Chris Curtis
Boris Zhukov and Nord the Barbarian beat Spike Jones and
  Chris Bassett
Scott Hall beat Earthquake Ferris

**FEBRUARY 7, 1986, SHOWBOAT SPORTS
PAVILION—LAS VEGAS**

Leon White beat Chris Curtis

FEBRUARY 9, 1986, MINNEAPOLIS TV

Mongolian Stomper and Boris Zhukov beat
  Earthquake Ferris and Woody Wilson
Stan Hansen beat Chris Curtis
Nord the Barbarian beat Mike Richards
Curt Hennig and Scott Hall beat Doug Somers and
  Spike Jones
Buck Zumhofe beat Chris Bassett

FEBRUARY 16, 1986, MINNEAPOLIS TV

Doug Somers beat Mike Richards
Scott Hall beat Chris Curtis
Bill Irwin and Scott Irwin beat Chris Bassett and
  Earthquake Ferris
Sgt. Slaughter, Jerry Blackwell, and Curt Hennig
  beat Boris Zhukov, Nord the Barbarian, and
  Mongolian Stomper

MAY 17, 1986, HAMMOND, INDIANA

Nick Bockwinkel beat Rick Gantner
Colonel DeBeers beat Chris Curtis
Buddy Rose and Doug Somers beat AWA tag team
    champions Scott Hall and Curt Hennig
Larry Zbyszko beat Larry Clark
Boris Zhukov beat Paul Barnett
Curt Hennig beat Kent Glover
AWA champion Stan Hansen beat Larry Clark
Midnight Rockers beat Brian Costello and Rick Gantner
Colonel DeBeers beat Earthquake Ferris
AWA tag team champions Buddy Rose and Doug Somers
    beat Dan Martin and Larry Clark
AWA champion Stan Hansen beat Kent Glover
Larry Zbyszko beat Chris Curtis
Nick Bockwinkel beat Kent Glover
Midnight Rockers beat Mad Maxx and Super Maxx

JUNE 10, 1986, SHOWBOAT SPORTS PAVILION— LAS VEGAS

Colonel DeBeers beat Chris Curtis

SEPTEMBER 19, 1986, MINNEAPOLIS TV

Greg Gagne beat Rick Gantner
AWA champion Nick Bockwinkel beat Rocky Stone
Scott Hall and Curt Hennig beat Earthquake Farris and
    Mike Tolos
Larry Zbyszko beat Chris Curtis
Sherri Martel beat Debbie Pelliter
Midnight Rockers and Jerry Blackwell beat Boris Zhukov,
    Nord the Barbarian, and Ali Khan

OCTOBER 12, 1986, SHOWBOAT SPORTS
PAVILION—LAS VEGAS

Scott Hall beat Tom Stone
Candi Devine beat Sherri Martel
Yuri Gordienko and Alexis Smirnoff beat Mike Richards
    and Frankie DeFalco
Johnny Rich beat Chris Curtis
Nick Bockwinkel beat Nord the Barbarian
Midnight Rockers beat Dennis Stamp and Tony Leone
Curt Hennig beat Larry Zbyszko

By now it should be obvious that anything can happen in professional wrestling. Surprises are part of the show, as is improvisa-
tion. During a match with Larry Zbyszko in 1986, he and I made
do with what we had to put on a good match. I loved working with
Zbyszko because he was one of the best heels in the business. He
used to insult the fans wherever he went, and in Milwaukee he
called the fans "spudheads." We were coming to the finish of our
match, and I'd just given Zbyszko a couple of backdrops, when
a guy in the audience held up a potato. I threw Zbyszko into the
corner, and he said to me, "Go get it." While Zbyszko was hanging
on the ropes, I climbed outside the ring and motioned for the guy
to give me the potato. The crowd went wild. I held up the potato
like I was asking them what to do with it. They pointed toward
Zbyszko and screamed. Still holding the potato, I got back in the
ring. Then Zbyszko said, "Hit me with it." The potato was pretty
hard, and while I was getting into the ring, I had been trying to
soften it up by squeezing it in my hand. I couldn't tell if it was soft
enough for me to hit Zbyszko with, so I grabbed his hair with
my left hand and used the potato to cover his forehead. Then I
smashed the potato on top of my hand, but the audience thought

I had smacked Larry with it! It was fantastic because the potato exploded into pieces and flew all over the ring. Zbyszko eventually made his comeback and pinned me, but the crowd was so into the match that they didn't care who won. I got cheers and backslaps all the way down the aisle toward the dressing room.

A few months later, I refereed a ladder match in Milwaukee between Scott Hall and Colonel DeBeers. During a ladder match, wrestlers use a ladder hidden under the ring to reach a bag of cash suspended over their heads. Before the match starts, someone has to go up the ladder and hang the bag. Guess who got *that* job? The crowd was yelling and screaming as I put a rickety sixteen-foot aluminum ladder in the ring and began to climb. My knees were shaking because I hate heights, and to make matters worse, I was holding a stupid paper bag with a big cartoon dollar sign on it that looked like a lame prop from the old *Batman* TV show. By the way, if anyone in the auditorium thought there was cash in that dopey-looking bag, they were not thinking straight. Verne Gagne wouldn't have put one dollar in there much less $20,000, or whatever amount was advertised. Anyway, with each step up, my legs shook more and more, and because I had to hold that stupid bag, I could only use one hand to steady myself. All the while, some bastard in the crowd kept yelling, "Don't fall, don't fall!" I

SEPTEMBER 19, 1986, MILWAUKEE AUDITORIUM—MILWAUKEE, WISCONSIN

Midnight Rockers beat AWA tag team champions
   Buddy Rose and Doug Somers (DQ)
Scott Hall beat Colonel DeBeers
Curt Hennig beat Mr. Go
Larry Zbyszko beat Chris Curtis
Sherri Martel beat Despina Montagas

wanted to kill him. I was drenched in sweat when Larry Lisowski, another AWA referee, finally showed up to help. Lisowski was a south Milwaukee firefighter and climbed ladders for a living, so he clipped the money bag to the rope, scrambled down, and we threw the ladder underneath the ring to get the match underway.

It was my job to keep the action moving. For the finish, Hall and DeBeers climbed the ladder at the same time, trading blows on the way up. Hall finally knocked DeBeers off the ladder and grabbed the prize money. I hope he was happy with his bag full of nothing. I know I was relieved when the whole thing was over!

I later found the guy who had taunted me while I was on the ladder. No one should be surprised that it was Larry Widen. But guess what? I got even with Widen when we stopped at Big Boy for a late dinner. While he was in the men's room, I ate his piece of pecan pie, whipped cream and all!

By 1987, it was clear that Verne Gagne had exhausted himself trying to keep the WWF from taking over his territory in the Midwest. The All-Star Wrestling house shows that were once on the cutting edge now looked dated in comparison to what McMahon was doing. Gagne couldn't match the big, multimedia bombast of smoke bombs and fireworks that accompanied a WWF main eventer's entrance. Wrestlers came out of the locker room to

---

**DECEMBER 6, 1986, MILWAUKEE AUDITORIUM—
MILWAUKEE, WISCONSIN**

Midnight Rockers and Despina Montagus beat Buddy Rose,
    Doug Somers, and Sherri Martel
AWA champion Nick Bockwinkel vs. Larry Zbyszko (NC)
Scott Hall beat Colonel DeBeers in a ladder match
Leon White beat Boris Zhukov
Curt Hennig drew Super Ninja
Earthquake Ferris beat Jerry Sagonowich

explosions, flashing lights, and signature rock music played at an earsplitting volume. Gagne knew I had to make a living, so he gave me his blessing to work for the WWF. A gentleman to the end, Gagne said he would continue to use me as much as possible.

Word soon got out that I was free to work for the AWA and the WWF. I started getting calls from Chief Jay Strongbow, a retired wrestler booking job men for McMahon. Strongbow said he had something for me in Indianapolis and that the pay was good. When I got to the arena, he came up to me and said, "Curtis, I got you wrestling Beefcake tonight." I had wrestled him before, back when he called himself Ed Boulder. When he joined the WWF, Boulder changed his name to Brutus "the Barber" Beefcake and added a great gimmick to his act. After Beefcake put his opponent in the sleeper hold, he cut a chunk of hair from the back of the guy's head.

When Strongbow said Beefcake wanted to cut my hair, I said it would be alright. "He'll just take a little snip out of the back and show it to the crowd, right?" I asked. Strongbow replied, "Well, yeah, that's the way he used to do it. But now we want to try something new." He added, "We'll pay you an extra $250 on top of your regular fee if you do it." I should have figured that something was up, because promoters never threw money away. I guess I only heard the part about the extra cash. Once I was in the ring with Beefcake, we locked up for a few moves before he put me in the sleeper hold. I went down like Sonny Liston in that famous picture on the cover of *Sports Illustrated*. While my eyes were closed, I felt some crap getting sprayed on my head, then I heard a buzzing sound. Jesse Ventura, Bruno Sammartino, and Vince McMahon Jr. were ringside. Sammartino and McMahon were the straight men, so all I could hear was Ventura saying, "Oh, now this is a real shame. Curtis is in there trying to do his best, and Beefcake has to treat him like this!" Ventura was always really funny, one of the greatest talkers ever.

Beefcake slapped me on the cheeks a couple times, signaling me that it was time to wake up. I opened my eyes and looked at

Beefcake holding a huge mirror. When I saw the bug row cut from the middle of my scalp, I sold the hell out of it. I flew backward, did a huge bump, and fell out of the ring. The crowd was laughing and catcalling as I ran into the dressing room. Back in the dressing room, the guys were clapping and cheering. "Curtis, you were so good tonight we're going to give you an extra $100," McMahon said. Then McMahon told Beefcake to cut all my hair off to the same length. Talk about being the guinea pig for one crazy idea!

Afterward, I called Jan and said, "I've got good news and bad news." She said, "You got hurt, right?" I said, "No. The good news is, I made almost $1000. The bad news is, I'm bald!" When I got home, Jan took one look at me and said, "If they ever ask you to do something stupid like that again, will you please say no?" For a month after, Jan refused to be seen in public with me unless I was wearing a baseball cap. Even my six-month-old daughter thought I looked funny. Remember, Jan hated wrestling. She liked the payouts, though.

I scored another victory in the ring when in 1987 I wrestled Ted "the Million Dollar Man" DiBiase in LaCrosse, Wisconsin. DiBiase walked around ringside throwing money to the fans before his matches. Before our match, DiBiase grabbed the microphone and announced that he didn't feel like wasting his time on a lowly jobber. He called out another wrestler, Mr. Washington, and handed him $5,000 to take his place. The announcers, Bobby Heenan and Gorilla Monsoon, went back and forth wondering if what DiBiase was doing was legal. Mr. Washington stuffed the wad of bills in his trunks and the match got underway. I didn't give him

**JUNE 23, 1987, MARKET SQUARE ARENA—
INDIANAPOLIS, INDIANA**

Brutus "the Barber" Beefcake defeats Chris Curtis

a chance. I knee-dropped Mr. Washington, then gave him plenty of punishment before pinning him in less than two minutes. Chalk up another victory for Chris Curtis! After the match, DiBiase and his valet, Virgil, roughed up Mr. Washington and took the money away from him. Heenan thought that was hilarious.

I loved working for the WWF because it was fun and Vince McMahon paid so well. Still, I hated to see my time with Verne Gagne and the AWA come to a close in 1991, when the AWA folded. If you add up the years I watched Gagne on TV and the years I worked for him, we had close to a twenty-five-year relationship.

As regional outfits such as the AWA gave way to the WWF, professional wrestling fell completely into Vince McMahon's control. When that happened, it just wasn't the same. New guys were doing high-risk, flashy, choreographed moves, and they were taking a lot of drugs to deal with the pain that came with injuries. Neither were the new guys classically trained wrestlers. Some saw their careers end by the time they were twenty-five or thirty years old. The older generation of professional wrestlers was giving way to a new one, and I could see that soon there wouldn't be a place for me in the sport.

Some people say professional wrestling isn't a sport. When I hear that, I just nod and walk away. In other sports, such as football, baseball, or basketball, the players have to trust their teammates or risk failure. Professional wrestling is no different, because pro wrestlers count on the fact that the other guys know what they're doing. Jobbers had to trust the stars to be pros. Stars had to trust the job men to put them over right and make them look good in the ring. Job men needed to trust the stars not to get them seriously injured. In many cases, the job man and the star never met before working together, so it was up to everyone in the business to be a professional and know exactly what to do.

One guy who really set the bar high as a professional wrestler

**JUNE 24, 1987, LOUISVILLE GARDENS—
LOUISVILLE, KENTUCKY**

Billy Jack Haynes, Hillbilly Jim, and Tito Santana beat
Chris Curtis, Terry Gibbs, and Tiger Chung Lee

**AUGUST 4, 1987, DANE COUNTY COLISEUM—
MADISON, WISCONSIN**

Koko B. Ware beat Chris Curtis

**AUGUST 5, 1987, LACROSSE CENTER—
LACROSSE, WISCONSIN**

Chris Curtis beat Mr. Washington

**SEPTEMBER 15, 1987, CIVIC
CENTER—PEORIA, ILLINOIS**

Ivan Putski and the Junkyard Dog beat Chris Curtis and
Mike Poland

**SEPTEMBER 16, 1987, METRO CENTER—
ROCKFORD, ILLINOIS**

The Heenan Family (Hercules, King Harley Race, and
King Kong Bundy) beat Brady Boone, Chris Curtis,
and Scott Casey

was Paul "Mr. Wonderful" Orndorff. I wrestled him in October
1987. Orndorff's signature finish was a jumping piledriver. To do
it, Orndorff bent the job man over, clamped his head between
his knees, jumped, and fell backward to the mat. A split second
before the moment of impact, Orndorff released his grip on the
job man's head. To the audience, it appeared that his opponent's
head was driven into the mat with near-lethal force, but in reality,
the job man got away unharmed.

As Orndorff and I went to the finish, I was fully aware that if for any reason my head hit the mat before Orndorff released me, I would be a quadriplegic for life. Orndorff gave me a straight-arm clothesline across the throat as I rebounded off the ropes, then he put me in the perfect position for what many called the most devastating piledriver in wrestling. My legs went straight in the air and I held onto his knees as Orndorff jumped. His butt hit the mat a millisecond before my head, which allowed me to simultaneously push up and out of the hold. I looked like a pogo stick as I bounced around before collapsing to the canvas. It was beautiful, because it looked like Orndorff had killed me! The crowd was screaming, and ringside commentators Jesse Ventura and Vince McMahon Jr. dropped their jaws in amazement. I shook my head and flopped around like I was having seizures. All the while, I was laughing because Orndorff had done the move so well. I never felt a thing.

I wrestled another great professional with a devastating finisher the next day in Green Bay. The six foot four, 320-pound Killer Khan finished his matches by body slamming his opponent to the mat and temporarily blinding him by spitting green mist in his eyes. While his opponent was blinded, Khan would climb the top rope and jump off, landing with his knee across the guy's chest. Having been on the receiving end of one version or another of this move, I can tell you that the key to not getting hurt or killed is to remain completely still. As Khan came off the top rope toward me, I willed myself to stay stiff as a board, praying for an instant death if Khan wasn't able to hold back. Khan's knee barely grazed my chest, but I sold the move to make it look like Khan had really hurt me.

I had to experience a less dangerous but no less terrifying finisher when I wrestled Jake "the Snake" Roberts in Cape Girardeau, Missouri, in March 1988. That night, I knew I was in for one of the most unusual bouts of my career. Roberts came to the ring with a burlap sack, inside of which was a ten-foot boa constrictor named

OCTOBER 6, 1987, MILWAUKEE ARENA— MILWAUKEE, WISCONSIN

Paul Orndorff beat Chris Curtis

OCTOBER 7, 1987, BROWN COUNTY VETERANS MEMORIAL ARENA—GREEN BAY, WISCONSIN

Killer Khan beat Chris Curtis

NOVEMBER 19, 1987, ESPN SHOWBOAT SPORTS PAVILION—LAS VEGAS

Lance Allen and Stoney Burke vs. the Original
   Midnight Express
Rick Gantner vs. Steve Olsonoski
Tommy Rich beat Chris Curtis
Billy Anderson vs. Boris Zhukov

JULY 2, 1987, ESPN SHOWBOAT SPORTS PAVILION—LAS VEGAS

Lance Allen vs. Mitch Snow
Soldat Ustinov and Boris Zhukov beat Billy Bold Eagle and
   Chris Curtis
Jim Evans vs. Adrian Adonis and Paul E. Dangerously
Steve Olsonoski and Jerry Blackwell vs. the Original
   Midnight Express
Mike Tolos vs. Greg Gagne
Rocky Stone vs. Kevin Kelly and Madusa
Art Washington vs. Tommy Rich
Steve Olsonoski beat Chris Curtis
Jim Evans and Stony Burke vs. the Original Midnight
   Express and Paul E. Dangerously

Damien. The crowds loved Jake the Snake, and Roberts's popularity at one time nearly matched Hulk Hogan's. The audience was always in full throat as a heel was on the mat helping Roberts sell his big finish, when Roberts let Damien out of the bag to slither on his victim.

I attacked Roberts from behind to start the match. Later, he took control when he stopped me with a big clothesline. Then he looked at the crowd and twirled his index finger in a circular motion to signal what was coming. Roberts grabbed me in a front lock and slammed me headfirst into the mat. His butt hit the canvas before I did, giving me a chance to protect my head from injury. Just as it had to be with Orndorff's piledriver, the timing with Roberts's move had to be perfect or the finish would look really bad. Roberts locked me in, and as we went down, my right hand hit the mat just before my head. I never felt a thing, but to the audience it looked like Roberts had planted me six feet under!

Once I was down, Roberts shouted at the crowd and urged them on. When he tossed Damien on my chest, the audience screamed in approval. On the commentary, Vince McMahon Jr. said Damien looked like he'd gained some weight, possibly from swallowing another job man during the first taping. Jesse Ventura said it looked like Damien was trying to kiss me. That damn Jesse!

As I've said, sometimes the moves didn't hurt as much as they looked like they did. Sometimes, though, what went on in the ring hurt like hell. When I got in the ring with Wahoo McDaniel in Las Vegas in 1988, I was in for a real beating. McDaniel was one of the all-time great wrestlers. In 1988, he was also in charge, along with Ray Stevens, of running television matches. When I found out I was working with McDaniel, I thought it was okay because I had ten years in the business and had wrestled a lot of tough guys. Plus, McDaniel knew who I was. We didn't even go over the match.

**MARCH 19, 1988, SHOW ME CENTER—
CAPE GIRARDEAU, MISSOURI**

Jake Roberts beat Chris Curtis

**MAY 10, 1988, ENTERTAINMENT CONVENTION
CENTER—DULUTH, MINNESOTA**

Sam Houston and the Fabulous Rougeaus
    (Jacques Rougeau and Raymond Rougeau) beat
    Chris Curtis, Danny Davis, and Pete Sanchez

**MAY 11, 1988, MAYO CIVIC CENTER—
ROCHESTER, MINNESOTA**

Jim Duggan beat Chris Curtis

**JUNE 25, 1988, ESPN SHOWBOAT SPORTS
PAVILION—LAS VEGAS**

Curt Hennig vs. David Koorijion
Wahoo McDaniel vs. Pete Sanchez
Jerry Lawler beat Chris Curtis

**JULY 2, 1988, ESPN SHOWBOAT SPORTS
PAVILION—LAS VEGAS**

Jerry Lawler beat Chris Curtis
Badd Company vs. Robert Gibson and Greg Gagne

That night, we did one high spot before McDaniel locked me up and dragged me to a corner. Once I was pinned into the corner, McDaniel hit me with four open-handed chops to my chest. It felt like he was hitting me with a barber's leather belt. I didn't dare try blocking them or McDaniel would have beaten me to a bloody mess. As McDaniel kept hitting me, Lee Marshall, the ringside announcer, was beside himself. Then McDaniel fired me into the opposite turnbuckle. At the last second, I made a decision to take the hit harder than I ever had before. I hit the turnbuckle so hard that the ring moved six inches. Finally, McDaniel threw me into the ropes for a reverse tomahawk chop, then a double underhook suplex for the big finish.

Just as I had done with lots of others, I made McDaniel look like a great wrestler that night. It's what I got paid to do as a job man, and I loved every second of it.

JULY 9, 1988, ESPN SHOWBOAT SPORTS PAVILION—LAS VEGAS

Wahoo McDaniel beat Chris Curtis
Badd Company vs. Pete Sanchez and Mike Lucca
Mando Guerrero vs. Brian Costello

JULY 13, 1988, LA CROSSE CENTER— LA CROSSE, WISCONSIN

The British Bulldogs (Davey Boy Smith and the Dynamite Kid) beat Chris Curtis and Tom Burton
The Hart Foundation (Bret Hart and Jim Neidhart) beat Chris Curtis and Tom Stone

JULY 14, 1988, FIVE SEASONS CENTER— CEDAR RAPIDS, IOWA

Ken Patera beat Chris Curtis

JULY 16, 1988, ESPN SHOWBOAT SPORTS PAVILION—LAS VEGAS

Cousin Luke beat Chris Curtis
Soldat Ustinov and Teijho Kahn vs. Larry Bicone and David Koorijion
The Top Guns (Ricky Rice and Derrick Dukes) vs. Pete Sanchez and Brian Costello
The Road Warriors vs. the Fabulous Ones

OCTOBER 6, 1988, SPORTS ARENA—
TOLEDO, OHIO

Jim Powers beat Chris Curtis

JANUARY 20, 1989, MILWAUKEE AUDITORIUM—
MILWAUKEE, WISCONSIN

The Top Guns beat Chris Curtis and Tony Leone
Larry Zbyszko beat Jim Evans
Wahoo McDaniel beat the Menace
Mean Mike Enos beat Billy Bold Eagle
The Top Guns beat Steve Butler and Pete Sanchez
Colonel DeBeers beat Jim Evans
Tommy Jammer beat Tony Leone
Brad Rheingans beat Chris Curtis
Mando Guerrero and Hector Guerrero beat Steve Butler
    and Jake Milliman
Larry Zbyszko beat Billy Bold Eagle
Wendi Richter beat Awesome Ondy Austin
Greg Gagne beat Chris Curtis

APRIL 26, 1989, CIVIC CENTER—
OMAHA, NEBRASKA

The Bushwhackers (Butch and Luke) beat Barry Horowitz
    and Chris Curtis

MAY 16, 1989, LA CROSSE CENTER—
LA CROSSE, WISCONSIN

The Bushwhackers beat Al Burke and Chris Curtis

MAY 17, 1989, ENTERTAINMENT CONVENTION
CENTER—DULUTH, MINNESOTA

The Rockers beat Chris Curtis and Jake Milliman

**JUNE 6, 1989, DANE COUNTY COLISEUM—
MADISON, WISCONSIN**

WWF World Tag Team Championship: Demolition
(Ax and Smash) beat Chris Curtis and Tom Stone

Chapter 7

Though I was still wrestling for the WWF in the late 1980s, I knew that eventually I would have to do something else if I wanted to stay in the business. The best way I could figure to do that was to pass the knowledge and skills I had acquired over ten years in the industry onto up-and-coming wrestlers. No matter how flashy or theatrical Vince McMahon Jr.'s shows became, the WWF would still need job men who knew what they were doing.

I opened Curtis Pro Wrestling Camp on July 5, 1989. I hired a jobber named Al Burke to help me conduct training sessions three days a week. Burke had gotten into wrestling a year or two before I did, and we shared an interest in turning out job men who knew the trade.

My business was located at Sixth Street and Lincoln Avenue in Milwaukee. All were welcome, but I auditioned every potential student, sizing up their natural abilities in the process. I discouraged anyone who didn't weigh at least two hundred pounds from enrolling, simply because it was unlikely they would find work at a lighter weight.

Curtis Pro Wrestling Camp wasn't cheap. I charged $1,000 for a three-month course. Attendees were given thorough instruction as well as advice designed to help them avoid making the same mistakes I had made when I was new to the business. Graduation did not guarantee a career in wrestling, but the students who made it through got a shot at a TV match. After that, they had to show the promoters they could stay in the game. One of my best

A newspaper ad for my pro wrestling camp. *MILWAUKEE JOURNAL SENTINEL*

students was Mike Richards, who found success as a member of the heel tag team the Texas Hangmen.

One day, a writer from the *Milwaukee Journal Sentinel* stopped in and expressed interest in doing a piece for the paper. He watched some training sessions before asking me, "Is this stuff for real?" I got a little hot under the collar, but kept my cool. I replied, "Everyone's entitled to their own opinion, but sportswriters who criticize wrestling have never been in the ring. They have no idea what it's like." I went on to say that while it's the showmanship that draws fans and brings in the money, wrestling still needs physicality, athleticism, and ability to be effective. Then I told the reporter, "Anyone who thinks it's playtime in that ring can ask my wife about how many bruises I have or about the days when it takes me fifteen minutes to get out of a chair!" Burke chimed in with a great point. "You never hear another pro athlete badmouth wrestling," Burke said.

Working out with Al Burke at my wrestling school in 1989. *MILWAUKEE JOURNAL SENTINEL*

A few weeks after the article on my camp ran in the *Journal*, I got a call from a woman in Los Angeles who said she worked for Pat Sajak, the host of *Wheel of Fortune*. I said, "Yeah, right," and hung up. She called back and convinced me she wasn't a prank caller. CBS had recently launched a new late-night talk show hosted by Sajak, and the producers wanted to know if I'd come on the show and talk about wrestling. They also wanted me to bring someone to help demonstrate the various moves and holds.

It turned out to be a first-class experience from beginning to end. Mike Richards and I flew to Los Angeles where we were met by a chauffeur holding up a sign with my name on it. The limo took us to the Avalon Hotel in Beverly Hills. All the rooms were little cabanas that surrounded a huge swimming pool. The palm trees and other landscaping shielded the whole complex from the street, so it was very private and very swanky.

When the representative from Sajak's show called to give me the itinerary for the next day's taping, she said we should have dinner and look around Los Angeles, and they'd pick up the cost. Richards and I walked over to Hamburger Hamlet on Beverly

Drive near Wilshire. After dinner, Richards and I took a cab to Hollywood Boulevard. He wanted to do some shopping, so I went to see Michael Douglas in *Black Rain*. Later I walked to the Roosevelt Hotel and had a couple drinks at the bar. Classic old Hollywood all the way.

The next morning, a limo took us to the CBS studios at Television City in Hollywood. The chauffeur drove past the back lot with movie sets and various streets that looked like New York, the Old West, and small-town America. We were escorted to the new second-floor studio where the Sajak show was filmed. Richards and I got into our wrestling gear, and an aide moved us to the green room, where guests of the show could relax before they went on. Actress Jill Clayburgh was in there, along with actor Danny Aiello. Aiello was really nice, but Clayburgh acted like she was too good to be sitting there with professional wrestlers.

When it was our turn to go on, I talked with Sajak, and then Richards and I went over a couple of basic moves. During a commercial break, Sajak changed into a leopard skin outfit that looked like it had been worn in an old Tarzan movie. Sajak climbed in the ring and I put him in a few holds. Then I bench pressed him over my head and started to give him the airplane spin. The producer and a couple of Sajak's handlers were just off camera, and I could them saying, "Don't hurt him, please, don't hurt him!" Sajak isn't a very big guy, so there was no way I was going to hurt him. I gently set him down. When it was all over, Richards and I flew home with our expenses paid and $550 each in our pockets.

Through it all, I kept wrestling, though I did so at smaller venues. In 1995, I promoted a card of my own held at St. John's Cathedral High School on the Milwaukee School of Engineering campus. I hired Jim Brunzell, Buck Zumhofe, and the Texas Hangmen for the card. Steve Hall wore a Dr. X look-alike mask for his bout. Brunzell was sick and didn't make it to the show, but I was very proud to have Mike Richards, my former student and successful wrestler, there for a match.

An ad for one of the cards I promoted in 1996. *MILWAUKEE JOURNAL SENTINEL*

APRIL 3, 1998, GERMANTOWN HIGH SCHOOL—
GERMANTOWN, WISCONSIN

Chris Curtis vs. Jon Paige

JUNE 28, 1998, SUMMERFEST CELLULAR ONE
SPORTS AREA—MILWAUKEE, WISCONSIN

Twelve-man battle royal with Chris Curtis, Trevor Adonis,
Colonel Corruption, Haystacks Ross, Mike Anthony,
and David Herro

Around this time, I returned to my roots. I went back to wrestling in beer halls, at fireman's picnics, and at county fairs. I was getting older and had accomplished nearly everything I'd set out to do when I broke into professional wrestling, so I was comfortable working smaller shows. I do have a regret or two, though. I would have loved to wrestle at Madison Square Garden in New York City, the most famous arena in the world. I also wish I could have wrestled the Crusher and Verne Gagne. Otherwise, I have no complaints. I had a long and satisfying career, and I feel blessed.

By 2003, my body had started to tell me that it was time to call it quits. At forty-six years old, it had become tough for me to roll out of bed. A few main-event stars I knew were still wrestling in their sixties, which made no sense to me.

Then, in 2014, I got a call from Jeff Frank, the artistic director of Milwaukee's First Stage Children's Theater. Frank had learned about me through Larry Widen, whose kids, Joe and Emily, had been involved in various productions at the theater for more than ten years. Frank told me the theater was producing an original play about Mexican wrestling called *Luchadora*. Written by Alvaro Saar Rios, a University of Wisconsin–Milwaukee professor, *Luchadora* is about empowering women. A young girl named Lupita finds a wrestling mask and a suitcase while rummaging around in her grandma's attic. She learns her father was a wrestler, and she wants to honor his name by following in his footsteps. Frank gave me a script and asked me to help construct the finale in which Lupita takes on the heel, El Hijo. I told him the most important aspect of professional wrestling is to keep the audience guessing and never tip your hand until the last minute. Frank wondered if I'd serve as the play's wrestling consultant, and I happily said I would.

In February 2015, I started showing the kids the fundamentals of wrestling. I brought my son, Joe, along to help with the first workout. Joe was a varsity heavyweight wrestler at Germantown High School and a two-time state qualifier in his junior and senior years. He finished his career with 108 wins, 70 by pinfall. He's ranked as one of the best heavyweight wrestlers in Germantown history. After graduation, Joe did a year in MMA submission wrestling. When we walked into the theater to meet the cast and crew, the look in their eyes was priceless! I'm 285 pounds, and Joe is 290 pounds. I'm sure they all thought, "Why did I sign up for this? Why?" As we were introduced to everyone, I told them that I wasn't there to toss anyone over the top rope but to teach them how to fall safely and make the wrestling scenes look authentic. It was my job to protect the kids' health and safety, and I promised them I would never ask them to perform dangerous stunts. We did a thirty-minute nonstop assembly line of body locks, hip throws, and the fireman's carry headlock takedown. The kids were pretty sore, but they loved it.

Frank and I scripted out moves for the big finish in which El Hijo puts the claw hold on Lupita. She sinks to the mat, then, out of nowhere, her father shows up and cheers her on to victory. I tried to keep it simple, but Frank wanted something dramatic that would really put Lupita over. I came up with a gem! El Hijo has the claw on Lupita when over the sound system you hear, "She

Luchadora playbill. I was the fight choreographer and showed the young actors how to safely perform the wrestling scenes. FIRST STAGE CHILDREN'S THEATER

drank the whole thing!" Earlier, Lupita drinks an elixir that gives her enough strength to get back on her feet. She breaks the claw hold and hip-tosses El Hijo. Finally, she applies an arm bar to El Hijo, and he taps out. The suspense in the finish was inspired by a hero of mine, the great wrestler Dusty Rhodes.

Jeff and Alvaro loved it, and the casts did a magnificent job performing their moves. The production crew was wonderful to work with, and I went away feeling great. It was an ending to my wrestling career that I never expected.

Acknowledgments

My thanks go to the late Verne Gagne for everything he did for me during my ten years at the American Wrestling Association. Gagne, along with his son, Greg Gagne, and Wally Karbo, who has since passed away, ran the greatest organization in the history of the sport. I was helped by so many other people who worked there as well. Nick Bockwinkel and Ray Stevens were great mentors who encouraged me to keep trying when I wasn't sure if I could cut it in the business. Their objective critiques of my matches made me a better wrestler. And Bobby Heenan, the greatest heel, manager, and mouthpiece who ever stepped in the ring, was the reason I got into wrestling in the first place.

Baron von Raschke was a friend who participated in a card I promoted, and he was kind enough to write the foreword to this book.

Other wrestlers who took the time to help me include Tito Santana, whom I worked a number of times. During a match in Milwaukee, Tito showed me the finer points of working with a light touch. When I touched his hair, Tito did the rest, moving his head suddenly as if I had yanked it with all my strength. Ox Baker was another mentor who looked mean as hell but was really a three-hundred-pound cotton ball in the ring. Apache Bull Ramos was another friend who showed me how vital it was to protect the integrity of the business at all costs. When we drove to matches, he made me drop him off two blocks from the venue so the fans wouldn't catch a glimpse of us together. And Bob Sweetan told me how to protect myself from overzealous fans. "If you're outside the ring, get away from 'em fast or they'll sue ya," he said. "But if one of 'em so much as sticks his head inside the ring, you got the green light to knock his teeth out with a knee or an elbow."

Most of all, I am indebted to Steve Hall, who saw potential in me when I first broke into the business. His guidance and advice helped me develop skills and abilities to become a job man who gave everything he had in the ring.

Thanks also go to my ex-wife, Janice. She hated pro wrestling with a passion, but she put up with it for many years, and allowed me to tell some of the stories here.

And, finally, thank you to Ron and Barbara Multerer, my mom and dad. They weren't crazy about my career path, but they supported the choices I made. My dad enjoyed reading a draft of this book before he passed away. I only wish my mom would have lived long enough to do the same. I love you both.